SETTLIN ESTATES
ESTATES
for Everyone

SETTLING ESTATES

ESTATES

for Everyone

A Practical Guide and Action Plan to Handle Assets, Benefits, Taxes, Debts, Minors, and Much More

RONALD FARRINGTON SHARP

ALLWORTH PRESS
NEW YORK

Allworth Press books may be purchased in bulk at special discounts for sales promotion, corporate gifts, fund-raising, or educational purposes. Special editions can also be created to specifications. For details, contact the Special Sales Department, Allworth Press, 307 West 36th Street, 11th Floor, New York, NY 10018 or info@skyhorsepublishing.com.

26 25 24 23 22   5 4 3 2 1

Published by Allworth Press, an imprint of Skyhorse Publishing, Inc. 307 West 36th Street, 11th Floor, New York, NY 10018.

Allworth Press® is a registered trademark of Skyhorse Publishing, Inc.®, a Delaware corporation.

www.allworth.com

Cover design by Mary Belibasakis

Library of Congress Cataloging-in-Publication Data is available on file.

Print ISBN: 978-1-62153-789-2
eBook ISBN: 978-1-62153-790-8

Printed in the United States of America

Contents

Introduction

What needs to be done at the death of a loved one? There are four basic steps that must be followed. First is the arrangement for burial or cremation. Then the assets of the deceased have to be inventoried, followed by getting all debts paid and legal requirements met, followed by distributing the assets to the people who are supposed to get them according to the person's will, trust, or state law. The job can be daunting, expensive, and time-consuming—especially if the deceased had not made proper plans for the estate by setting up a will or trust beforehand. Settling a person's estate is something most people, other than lawyers, have never done. Help is right here.

This book is a guide for those responsible for wrapping up the personal and financial affairs of the deceased. It is not intended to address coping with the emotional issues of the loss or how to handle grieving. It is a resource identifying the steps that may need to be taken prior to and after a person's death. It is a practical guide to assist those who must deal with asset collection and disposition; tax and legal issues; applying for benefits such as Social Security, life insurance, veteran's benefits; debts; dealing with issues involving minor children; and employment benefit plans. With this book as a guide, the process of administering and wrapping up a deceased's estate will be much simpler.

The information in this book is not intended as a replacement for legal advice and is informational in intent. Laws and procedures vary from state to state and even among counties within a state. Federal laws and agencies have their own procedures, which also are in flux and subject to political change. Read and learn, but consult an attorney for legal advice.

CHAPTER ONE

If Death Is Imminent

The time to begin settling the estate of a loved one is when it is clear that death is imminent. Sometimes this is easily established if, for example, attending physicians have made a terminal prognosis. Or, due to poor health or medical circumstances, it appears that the medical prognosis is so poor that there is little likelihood of the person living much longer.

It maybe feels a bit inappropriate, but preparations that can be done now, while the person is still alive, can make the post-death procedures simpler and less time-consuming, which the loved one would likely want. What can be done depends upon whether the person is mentally competent as well as able and willing to participate in document creation and decision-making. This is important since establishing competency will likely quash any allegations that decisions made and documents created are invalid. An allegation of lack of mental acuity can be the basis for a will contest, undue influence charges, or efforts to invalidate pre-death gifts or to void contracts entered into by the allegedly incompetent person.

LEGAL INCAPACITY/MENTAL INCOMPETENCY

Sometimes it is crystal clear that, due to dementia or severe medical conditions, a person is not mentally capable of making rational decisions. Failure to recognize family members or respond to simple questions are sure signs of this condition.

I have had several instances of someone bringing a parent or other person in, explaining that the person wants to make a will. What I do is explain that because of lawyer/client privilege, I need to talk to Mom alone. I can then determine whether she is aware of what is happening, knows where she is, who her family members are, and so forth to determine whether she is competent or is being subjected to undue influence. In one case Mom said that she didn't know who that guy was that brought her to see me. I refused to take the case; the guy was mad. But I thought it likely that he took Mom to another attorney who would be willing to prepare the will.

Courts are often asked to rule on the legal incapacity of a person (also called mental incompetency, or advanced dementia), usually as part of a petition to appoint a guardian and conservator for medical and business decision-making. The process differs by state, but generally is started by the filing of a written request by an interested party with the court. The petitioner does not have to be a family member, and often the process is initiated by the local adult protective services agency. However, you as a family member can ask the court to have you named as the legal guardian and conservator. Even a concerned neighbor can file the petition in most states.

TEMPORARY GUARDIAN OF ADULT

Typically, the judge will appoint a temporary guardian to represent the allegedly incapacitated person, who personally visits the person and makes a written recommendation to the court. There will also be a psychological evaluation done by a medical professional who also prepares a written opinion and report. If the judge decides there is enough evidence to declare a person incompetent, then a guardian is appointed, as well as a conservator if there are assets that need to be managed. A guardian is in charge of the person while a conservator is in charge of the person's finances.

A court hearing is then scheduled at which the person appears, if possible, as well as those who have the right to object to the petition and have his or her own attorney to challenge the petition.

After considering all evidence, the court will either dismiss the petition or will grant it. If the petition is granted, the court will appoint a permanent guardian and conservator. Sometimes family members will compete for that role, in which case the judge decides who would be the most appropriate person.

POWERS OF ATTORNEY

The court process can be avoided if the incapacitated person has the right sort of documents in place that define mental incapacity and appoint decision-makers for health and business purposes if those conditions are met. These documents of course must have been signed before incapacity to be valid.

For business decision-making, the most common document is a so-called durable power of attorney. A power of attorney (POA) is merely a written document that allows you to give someone the authority to sign your name and act for you in all or some business or financial matters the same as if you were doing so yourself. These might be broad powers and include managing investment assets, writing and cashing checks, filing real estate documents, and tax returns. Or it might be limited to a particular purpose and for a limited amount of time, such as to represent you in a particular real estate transaction.

The important word is the "durable" part of the POA. Should you become mentally incompetent after signing the POA, then the person who has the power (often called your agent or attorney-in-fact) no longer has any authority to act for you since he can only do what you could legally do. Someone who is mentally incompetent has no legal ability to do things like sign contracts or checks or tax returns or anything else, and so neither would the person's agent under a normal power of attorney.

To get around this, the POA adds a provision that states that if you should be deemed incompetent according to the terms in the durable POA, then the agent still has the authority to act as your agent for all the defined purposes. *Durable* means the legal ability to act for you is valid even if you can't act for yourself.

In many cases the durable POA will specifically state that the agent never has any authority unless mental incapacity as defined actually occurs. We call that a springing durable power of attorney since it, "springs" into effect at that point.

The durable power of attorney may have language as follows, which defines mental incapacity for purposes of the POA:

> *Until I am certified as incapacitated as provided hereunder, this Power of Attorney shall have no force or effect. All authority granted in this Power of Attorney shall be subject to establishment of incapacity as provided hereunder. After this Power of Attorney becomes effective, it shall not be affected by any subsequent incapacity which I may hereafter suffer or the passage of time. For purposes of establishing incapacity, whenever two licensed, practicing medical doctors who are not related to me or to any beneficiary or heir at law by blood or marriage certify in writing that I am unable to manage my financial affairs because of mental or physical infirmity and the certificates are personally served upon me, then the attorney(s)-in-fact named herein shall assume all powers granted in this Power of Attorney.*
>
> *Anyone dealing with the attorney(s)-in-fact may rely upon written medical certificates or a photocopy of them presented to them along with the original Power of Attorney document, and shall incur no liability for any dealings with any designated attorney(s)-in-fact in good faith reliance on said certificate and the original Power of Attorney document. This provision is inserted in this document to encourage third parties to deal with my attorney(s)-in-fact without the need for court proceedings.*

The springing durable POA, if executed while the person is competent, obviates the need for a court-ordered guardianship and would likely be used as evidence in disputing the need for a court-appointed guardian. Courts however still have the ulti-mate authority, though the document will carry a lot of weight.

The other document that you should have is a medical power of attorney and designation of a patient advocate for medical decision-making. Many states have standardized forms for this purpose, but will recognize properly drafted documents that serve the same purpose.

Unfortunately, someone decided to name a health care directive a "living will." This is not a will. It is a statement of your wishes regarding your medical treatment in the event you are unable to communicate those wishes verbally to health care providers. It often directs what should be decided in an end-of-life scenario. If the deceased signed one of these and had no last will and testament, it means he or she died intestate. Without a will.

Note that a power of attorney will usually not give an agent the power to create a will or trust for you. Also—it should go without saying—at the death of the person who made the POA, the agent's authority ceases and the document is no longer valid.

It is a very good idea to have witnesses who can attest to the mental acuity at the time of signing the POA or other documents to forestall a challenge later on. Some attorneys actually record the signing, which includes a recorded statement by the signer to make it clear that she understands what she is doing and that it is voluntary and at her direction.

The lesson here is that everyone should have the two POAs just discussed to avoid court proceedings and discourage challenges.

If the person is mentally competent

Assuming the person is competent and is able and willing to work with you, it is important that you get information concerning the location and identification of all important documents and assets. The powers of attorney should also be prepared in case of later incapacity. I also suggest getting a list of those who should be notified at the time of death including fraternal organizations and the US Department of Veterans Affairs, since they offer services prior to and after death. More about this later.

If the person is reluctant to reveal all this information, we sometimes explain that if the assets are not found and not claimed then they will escheat to the state rather than going to the heirs. That usually does it, but there are some who refuse to talk about death planning for whatever reason. The best we can then do is ask that the assets, titles, locations, and passwords be written down and placed either with the family attorney or kept in a sealed envelope to be opened at death.

The checklist in the appendix highlights the most common types of assets that a person might own, but there may be others. Some clients own aircraft or shares in oil and gas leases. Passwords or account numbers for digital virtual currency like Bitcoin are sometimes impossible to find from any source other than the owner. I had a client who owned a long-term lease on a gold mine in Alaska, so ask questions about unusual assets. Getting passwords for computers, websites, and telephones is very important since these can be difficult to acquire otherwise. Email often contains information that is unavailable elsewhere. Nowadays going green means no paper statements are mailed. Bills for goods and services, utilities, insurance statements, brokerage and bank statements, and lots of other things are often sent only electronically. Monitoring the email as well as the snail mail is a valuable help for those who will later be in charge of the estate.

Lost or misplaced documents can be recreated while there is still time. Estate planning documents such as wills and trusts need to be collected and preserved. As an estate planning attorney, I get calls from relatives of deceased clients who cannot find the original documents I created and hope that I have them even thirty or more years later. The fact is that even if I had the documents, unless the client had kept in touch with me, I would have no way of knowing whether they had been intentionally destroyed or amended by another attorney.

The way around this problem is to either file the will or trust with the court (most states have procedures to hold a will or trust for safekeeping that are not public record) or give signed copies to the named executor, personal representative, or trustee.

If there is time, and no estate planning has been done, take care of that right away. Having a trust or other probate avoiding plan will be invaluable at the time of death. See my book *How to Avoid Probate for Everyone* for lots of options.

Aside from business and estate-planning documents, now is the time to discuss with the person and family members wishes and instructions as to funeral and burial arrangements, cremation if desired, prepaid funeral plans if any, and the location of family burial plots.

Organ donation should be discussed. Some states allow for a statement on a driver's license to give this permission. There is an online national registry that allows you to register as an organ donor online. It will redirect you to your state's registry and you will need to provide information such as your driver's license number or state identification number.

Another decision to be made that should be discussed is whether life support should be continued in an irreversible terminal condition situation. This is the "Do Not Resuscitate" form, sometimes called rather cavalierly a Pull-the-Plug form. These instructions can also be included in the person's living will. There are state-approved forms online for all fifty states, some quite lengthy, which can be used. A shorter, more generic form is included in Appendix G to this book, which I have seen used and honored by the medical community. However, an individual physician may refuse to follow the wishes of the decedent, in which case another physician or the hospital administration may have to be involved.

Not everyone should have this form. I personally do want to be resuscitated using CPR or other methods if I have a heart attack or some such thing. However, if a person is in a permanent vegetative state, being kept alive only by mechanical and medical means, there are many who prefer to be allowed to die rather than be kept alive artificially. But there are some who for personal reasons want to kept alive no matter what.

We can't argue with a person's personal preference. I am reminded, though, of a case where the husband was terminal with no real hope of recovery. He told me early on that he wanted to stay alive by any means since his pension paid much more while he was alive than his wife would get as a survivor's benefit. So, for him in his mind it made sense.

One issue that often arises is the disposition of personal property items such as collections, furnishings, jewelry, vehicles, and other "stuff." It's easy to say that everything should be divided equally, but one-of-a-kind items often cause more friction than does the cash.

If there are such items, have the person write down who gets what and the family will not likely contest it. This is something that can be included in a will or trust, but the real value is the desire of most to honor the written wishes of the deceased. More on that later.

I once held a protracted and expensive negotiation and even a court hearing over a dispute between a brother and sister about a multi-tool. This was a Swiss Army Knife sort of thing that was worth no more than fifty dollars, but they each claimed Dad wanted them to have it. In the end the brother ended up with it since it was in his possession when Dad died. Sister was not happy. There are a lot of other unhappy stories, such as the one brother of five who got to the house of the deceased before the others and removed all of Dad's expensive tools and firearms. The others grumbled about it but it didn't end up in court. Just lots of hard feelings and resentment.

CHAPTER TWO

Actions to Be Taken Immediately After Death

WHO IS IN CHARGE OF DECISIONS REGARDING POST-DEATH DECISION-MAKING?

The deceased may have prepared a will or trust to nominate one or more persons to be the personal representative or trustee. That nomination is followed absent court intervention. However, in family situations there is usually discussion and consent as to who will do the things that need to be done. This includes communication with medical providers, social workers, lawyers, tax professionals, funeral directors, and real estate brokers, as well as securing and maintaining properties, conducting inventories, and the other necessary tasks in settling an estate. It can be a time-consuming and difficult job and not one that everyone has the time to do. Tasks can be divided, but ultimately the court-appointed personal representative or trustee is the one who is responsible for overseeing the settlement of the estate.

ORGAN DONATION

If the deceased directed organ donation, it is important that the physicians attending at death know about this in advance. Many parts of a body are saved and transplanted to those in need. Estimates are that over 28,000 lives a year are saved because of organ donation. Kidneys, livers, lungs, hearts, corneas, and other organs can be saved if the medical staff is aware of the organ donation directive. While some medical conditions would bar a donation, such as HIV, diabetes, heart conditions, and blood disorders, the fact is that the demand for organ donations always exceeds the supply.

The consent to organ donation can be accomplished at the time the person renews a driver's license in most states. Or a simple form can be filled out and filed with the state organ donor registry. While there is no cost to making a donation, neither will anyone be paid for it.

All fifty states have adopted the 2006 Revised Uniform Anatomical Gift Act (UAGA), which allows for registration or driver license instruction of the organ donor intention and provides for the authority of the medical professionals to proceed with the removal of organs without the consent of the family. Many medical practitioners, however, will respect the wishes of the family if they object to the procedure.

If there was no document signed in advance of death, that is, no prior consent, the family may give such consent and the organ donation can proceed if the deceased is deemed a good candidate for such a procedure.

BODY DONATION

Leaving your body for medical science can be arranged in advance or, with the next of kin's permission, can be done with no advance planning soon after death. There are several organizations that can assist in this process, such as the United Tissue Network, MedCure, or Science Care. There is no cost or payment for this donation, but the facility will arrange ultimate cremation at no cost.

CREMATION

The instructions of the deceased as to cremation may be inserted in a will or in a signed medical directive. If there is no such instruction, the family can decide to take that route when it is legally permissible.

Arranging for the cremation involves getting a cremation certificate from the local governing authority. Typically, there is a twenty-four- to forty-eight-hour waiting period before the cremation can take place. Direct cremation is the least expensive but does not allow for a ceremony or viewing ahead of time. The body is put into the custody of the crematory and the costs are typically far less than a traditional funeral home arrangement. In fact, in most states funeral homes do not have to be involved at all. I am reminded of reading local newspaper advertisements while in Florida and seeing what amounted to a price war with competing crematory pre-arrangements. There is no need for a casket, burial vault, burial site, marker, or funeral home services, so the cost is significantly lower. There still may be additional fees for death certificates, an urn for the cremains, and miscellaneous fees for transporting the body and providing a flammable body container.

There are no firm rules as to what you may do with the cremains. They may be scattered with the permission of the landowner. Some prefer to have the urn stored in a niche in a mausoleum or placed in a container that can be buried in the same grave with a deceased spouse. There are other unusual services that include having the cremains incorporated into pottery, jewelry, even shot into space. It's up to you.

AUTOPSY

In cases of suspicious deaths, the state or county medical examiner may refuse to release the body until a definitive cause of death has been identified and stated on the death certificate. This is to leave the body available for forensic examination and autopsy in case of suspected homicide. Cremation would not be allowed without the consent of the coroner or medical examiner, depending upon the jurisdiction.

There are also situations also where the family might wish to have a private autopsy. In one case I handled, the deceased was found dead in his running car, which was parked in his garage with the door closed. The medical examiner quickly ruled the death a suicide, but the family strongly objected. There was a sizeable insurance policy on his life that would not be payable if it were suicide since the policy was recently taken out. We ordered a private autopsy that revealed that he had an extremely high blood-alcohol level. We theorized that he had arrived home, pulled in the garage, and passed out, then died of carbon monoxide inhalation. Ultimately, we forced the insurance company to pay.

In another case, not mine, the deceased died without any direct cause that could be identified other than heart failure. But the deceased had an ongoing medical malpractice case for improper diagnoses of bone cancer and unnecessary treatment via chemotherapy. The autopsy established that organ failure due to the chemo could have been a causative factor in the death, which was a help to the attorney handling the lawsuit.

TRANSPORTING DECEASED OVER STATE LINES

Cremated remains can be transported across state lines or even shipped with no problems provided they are in a sturdy sealed container. A body, however, involves other rules and considerable expense. The body has to be prepared for shipping, which means embalmed or refrigerated with dry ice. State laws vary and must be followed. Funeral homes are the best way to make these arrangements since they are familiar with the paperwork and processes that are entailed.

Bodies may be shipped via ground or can be sent as air freight. You should not try to make these arrangements yourself due to the complexities of the procedures. There have to be two funeral homes involved, the shipping one and the receiving one, each with its own duties and fees. The solution many choose is to have the body cremated in one state and shipped to the other state for the funeral.

It is possible in most states to deliver the prepared body yourself, thereby saving some transportation costs, but you will still need to have the body prepared for shipment through the funeral home.

WHO PAYS FOR FUNERAL
AND BURIAL EXPENSES?

This can be a contentious issue in families, particularly if there is no surviving spouse. If the deceased left no instructions, the type of arrangements, whether cremation or a full-blown funeral, will have to be decided among the family. Cost of course is a major concern for many, particularly if the deceased had modest or no assets to cover the expenses.

If there are assets in the name of the deceased or in his or her trust, then these assets are usually used for payment of estate expenses. Advance payment is typically required for any type of procedure, so someone has to step up to cover it. If someone pays the costs, then they are entitled to be first in line to be reimbursed from the estate. If there are insufficient assets to cover these costs but there is life insurance available, then the life insurance proceeds can be assigned in part to the funeral home with the consent of the beneficiary. Otherwise, a surviving spouse typically pays. If there is no surviving spouse and there is a probate case opened, then all death-related expenses are considered priority and are paid out of the person's estate prior to any distribution of assets to heirs or attorneys. If assets are in a trust to avoid probate, then the trustee will take care of payment using trust assets.

In indigent cases the local municipality or department of social services may have funds available. If the deceased is a veteran there are various expenses and services that Veterans Affairs will provide. (More about that in a later chapter.) Nowadays, in some cases crowdfunding is available to help cover these costs for a surviving family.

PLANNING THE FUNERAL

There are many decisions to be made regarding how a funeral should be conducted. Open casket or closed? How much visitation will precede the actual ceremony? Who will give the eulogy? Is embalmment desired or necessary? What about funeral clothing? Will there be a separate church-located service? Will any organizations such as Veterans Affairs or the Freemasons participate? Will there be a separate graveside service? What will the obituary say?

These questions and more arise. And we have to see whether the deceased had left specific instructions for the family as to one or all of these questions. It is important that the family be involved or at least be invited to participate in the planning. Some wishes might be impossible or difficult to grant. For example, I had a client who wanted inserted in her will a direction that she be buried in the cemetery that is closest geographically to Hartwick Pines State Park in Michigan. She had no idea where that might be, but said the family would just have to figure it out. And there was the guy who wanted a "Viking Funeral" where he would placed on a funeral pyre on a raft, set ablaze, and pushed out to sea. That family did the best they could to follow the instructions by having the guy cremated first and then setting the urn on the raft, which was set alight and pushed from the shore. They then retrieved the charred wood. Close enough.

FUNERAL COSTS; THE FTC FUNERAL RULE

Funerals are expensive because there are so many add-on costs besides the cost of a casket. And caskets are like cars in that they range from a no-frills basic model to a luxury all-bells-and-whistles highly expensive one. I have had to make funeral arrangements for a half dozen people and have endured the "sales talk" from the funeral home directors.

The Federal Trade Commission (FTC) has promulgated a series of rules regulating funeral practices to deal with unscrupulous practices some funeral directors once used. In Appendix D is a copy of regulations that were current as of 2020.

You are entitled to an itemized breakdown of the costs of the funeral services. They must give you these costs by telephone if you like, and must provide you with a printed list if you desire. Also, they must give you these estimated costs whether you are asking in advance on a pre-need basis or at the time of need.

Here is a copy of the itemized listing which must be provided. The dollar amounts listed are typical, not provided by the FTC, and are set by the funeral home, which means they will vary. You are not required to accept all of them unless that service is required by law. For example, a burial vault is not required by law in any state, but individual cemeteries may have their own rule that would require a vault or liner in which the casket is placed. Embalming is also not a requirement unless the body is being transported across state lines in some cases. Keep in mind too that these are the required disclosures for the items or services rendered, but the funeral home may have additional services to offer which would also be disclosed on the form.

You might also ask about "Immediate or Direct Burial," which eliminates most of the costs since there would be no memorial services, just the funeral home fee and the costs of burial.

FUNERAL PRICING CHECKLIST

"Traditional," full-service burial or cremation. (This is only an example and the fees listed are just to give you an idea of what you will see when you request an estimate from the funeral director. It should be clear how fast the costs can add up.)

Basic services fee for the funeral director and staff	$2,200
Pickup of body	375
Embalming	800
Other preparation of body	300
Least expensive casket	2,500
Description, including model # _____	
Outer Burial Container (vault)	1,600
Description _____	
Visitation/viewing — staff and facilities	425
Funeral or memorial service — staff and facilities	550

Graveside service, including staff and equipment	400
Hearse	350
Other vehicles (car to transport family to cemetery)	150
Other services:	
Cosmetics, makeup, dressing	300
Separate church service with casket/flowers	400
Arranging transportation of the body between funeral homes	2,500
Total _____	

Cemetery/Mausoleum Costs

Cost of lot or crypt (if you don't already own one)

Perpetual care

Opening and closing the grave or crypt

Grave liner, if required

Marker/monument (including setup)

It is a very good idea to get at least three estimates since you can then compare the costs using the written itemized lists they must provide to you.

PREPAID FUNERAL CONTRACTS: PROS AND CONS

Paying for your funeral in advance of death has several advantages. It takes the burden off your family in having to make the funeral-related decisions in a time of mourning. It also relieves the family of much of the financial burdens since funerals can be very expensive. You get to decide what type of funeral you want, such as an immediate burial or even cremation, and most of the costs will be covered.

A prepaid plan is in effect an insurance contract with the funeral home as the beneficiary. There are several ways the contract can be set up, including an actual insurance policy or a trust. The idea is that at your death the funeral home has already been paid for most—but not all—of the funeral costs. The contract will specify which costs are covered and which are not. Cemetery charges, for example, like opening and closing the grave, the cost of the lot, the headstone, and other fees are not usually part of the contract.

Several problems can occur with a prepaid plan. The funeral home might go out of business or, depending on the type of contract, they might embezzle the funds—which has happened. It could be that you end up living or dying in another locality far from the funeral home. Some contracts require that you use a particular cemetery for the burial, and most of the contracts are not transferable. (Michigan is the only state that I know of that requires that the contract be transferable.) Also, most are not cancelable without a penalty if you change your mind. Further, once the contract is in effect, you may not be able to make changes to your plans.

For the purposes of this book, the job of the family is to determine whether a prepaid plan exists, read it carefully, then discuss it with the insurance company or the funeral home to determine what expenses are covered and which are not. Look for clauses that allow the funeral home to raise the prices to current levels. The prepayment might turn out to be just a down payment. If you have issues with the contract or the funeral home, it is worth discussing with an estate attorney.

A better alternative to look at is purchasing burial or final expense insurance from an insurance company. The beneficiary would not be the funeral home; it would be one or more of your family members, or it can be paid to your estate or your revocable trust. There is typically no medical qualification needed and the company cannot cancel the policy or reduce benefits so long as the policy premiums are paid. Any excess policy proceeds over the funeral costs would then go to your family and not the funeral home.

OBITUARY

The obituary is the last statement about a person's life. How it is written should be a family decision. The funeral home can assist in writing a standard obituary, but having the family participate and suggest edits makes the obituary more personal.

However you write it, a consideration nowadays is where to send it to be published. The local newspaper is the customary first choice, but local print papers are ceasing publication one after another. There are online registries such as Legacy.com where current obituaries can be registered. And even the obituaries from defunct newspapers are being archived in digital form by various websites. Some choose to publish the obit in every local paper where the deceased had lived. Famous and newsworthy people are often listed in major papers like the *New York Times* and biographized in Wikipedia. Funeral homes will offer, for a fee, to print the obit on so-called memorial cards sealed in plastic as keepsakes for distribution to family and mourners or both.

DEATH CERTIFICATES

The funeral home or crematory will arrange for ordering certified copies of death certificates. You should ask for at least a dozen since they will be needed by various insurance companies, creditors, and governmental authorities. Extras can go to family members if desired. Hold on to a few since situations may arise long after the funeral where you need proof of death and cause of death. The information needed for the death certificate will be provided by family. Some of the information might be difficult to find if the surviving family is small. See the Form Letters and Sample Forms section for a form that can be used to provide the needed information. Here are the items needed in order for the death certificate to be completed:

- Legal Name—First, Middle, Last
- Gender
- Social Security Number
- Date of Death
- Date of Birth
- Age at Death
- Birth City, County, State, Country
- Armed Forces (Y/N)

- Maiden Name
- Last Residence—Address, Zip, City, County, State, Country
- Surviving Spouse, If Any—First, Middle, Maiden name, Last
- Father's First Name, Middle, Last
- Mother's First Name, Middle, Maiden
- Occupation
- Education Level
- Ethnicity

There are other parts of the certificate that are filled in by the attending physician or medical examiner, who will certify it and state the cause of death.

The certificate is typically available a few days after death unless there is an autopsy or in case of a suspicious or unexplained death. It is sometimes possible to get a temporary death certificate in a case where the cause of death has yet to be determined. This can serve to make insurance claims and open estate administration through the courts. The cause and manner of death section will just say "pending investigation."

As to cremations, the medical examiner's Cremation Approval Form or similar document will be needed before a body can be released for cremation. This should not take long provided that the death was not suspicious.

You should read the death certificate carefully. Errors can be corrected by requesting and paying for an amended death certificate. The person providing the cause of death, whether it be the coroner, medical examiner, or attending physician, may not have even seen the body, relying instead on information provided by investigating law enforcement officers, or medical or nursing home staff.

Deaths of the elderly that occur at home are often not investigated at all or reported to the coroner or medical examiner. The person's physician can certify the cause of death for the death certificate based on past medical history. Investigations have revealed a high incidence of incorrect information on elderly death certificates as to cause of death. Often it is stated as "natural causes," which can encompass a host of causes that are natural and are not suicide, accident, or homicide.

CHAPTER THREE

Who's in Charge of the Estate and Who Does What?

DIVIDING RESPONSIBILITIES; POWER OF ATTORNEY NO LONGER VALID

With the funeral over, it is now time to settle the estate. But who is in charge of doing the many things that need to be done? If the deceased left a will, then the personal representative (executor) named in the will is the responsible person. If there was also a trust, the trustee named in the trust is the one. Sometimes the deceased names more than one person for those roles, which is great if they get along. If they disagree and there is no tiebreaker direction in the documents, then the probate court might have to be asked to solve the issues.

If there was no trust and no will, then the probate court will, on the petition of an interested party, appoint a personal representative (PR) to take charge of the estate matters by issuing Letters of Authority so that the appointed person has written authorization to wrap up the estate.

The titles given to those acting on behalf of an estate can vary, though the duties are the same. Letters of Administration, Letters Testamentary, Executor, and Administrator are used in various courts to refer to the person in charge of an estate. For our purposes I will use PR for Personal Representative.

Normally the interested person is a surviving spouse or adult child of the deceased. That person typically contracts with a lawyer to prepare the necessary starting paperwork, attend court hearings, and prepare the final accountings and authorization for final distribution of estate assets. In most states an interested party can legally handle the probate process without a lawyer (some states do not allow this). But the fact is that the lawyers know what needs to be done and can make the process run more smoothly than can a layperson.

Remember that your power of attorney is no longer valid once the person who made it dies.

There is no preference given to the oldest child if more than one child wants to be the personal representative. If there are competing parties, a court hearing will be necessary for the judge to appoint someone. If there is no one in the family able and willing to act as the personal representative, the court can appoint a public administrator, typically a local attorney, to act as the PR. The administrator's fees are paid from the estate assets along with any estate or death taxes, inventory fees, appraisers, and guardian ad litem's fees if necessary.

As stated earlier, all these fees, attorneys, and the time it takes for court hearings and such are mostly eliminated if the deceased has made and funded a trust or used other probate avoiding methods—as set out in my books *Living Trusts for Everyone* and *How to Avoid Probate for Everyone*.

PERSON NAMED AS EXECUTOR/PERSONAL REPRESENTATIVE/TRUSTEE REFUSES TO ACCEPT THE JOB

What if someone is named in a will or trust as the PR or trustee and they don't want to do it? It is a paying position but can be a lot of work and might require taking time off from a job to meet with attorneys, bankers, investment folks, auctioneers, and real estate people. You are doing no one a favor by naming him or her as the PR. It is a favor that person is doing for you. The answer is that even though you are nominated, you can decline—you don't have to do it. I have had a number of people do exactly that once they found out their services were not required by law. The declination of trust, as it is called, puts the matter into the hands of the court unless the deceased had nominated second or third choices—a practice which I recommend.

There are some attorneys who will offer to perform all the duties of the PR by having the nominated person sign over a power of attorney so the actual PR would have few actual duties to perform. I do not recommend this unless money is no object since the attorney will be charging hourly attorney rates for even nonlegal matters. And much of the work to settle an estate is not legal work.

PRs are typically compensated for the work they do. While a fixed percentage of the estate is sometimes used to determine compensation, a more reasonable and easier to justify method is to have the PR keep time sheets detailing what was done, when it was done, and how much time it took to do something. Then the person's normal hourly rate for their occupation is multiplied by the number of hours worked to arrive at the PR fee. Judges like that, though I have seen them adjust the hourly rate if they think it is unreasonable.

LOCK THE HOUSE, FEED THE DOG: PRESERVING THE ASSETS

If there is a surviving spouse who continues to live in the marital home, then securing the deceased's assets is not much of a concern. In most cases the survivor inherits everything, so things like changing the locks and canceling credit cards to prevent unauthorized use are not necessary. There are exceptions, however. If the survivor has adult stepchildren and there is no will or trust, and there are assets which are not jointly owned marital property, the potential for conflict exists.

Pets. When death occurs, someone has to take care of the dog, cat, goldfish, and parrot. I had a close friend who instructed that I have her cat put down when the time came. I didn't do it and instead took the cat home with me until I could find it a permanent placement. There are no-kill shelters that will take the pets to try to re-home them. You can use social media to put out a call for adoption, which often works if you include a cute photo of Fluffy.

Stepchildren. Stepchildren sometimes take a proprietary interest in assets their parent brought into the second marriage. Not just money, but personal property items such as collections and heirlooms from the deceased parent's lineage are often expected to "stay in the family." Before the death of the first spouse the children of both likely did not interfere at all with how the couple's assets were used. At the death of one of them though the family bond might no longer exist and fear and greed can cause people to make claims they never would have asserted previously.

In one case the house was supposed to go to the surviving spouse, but no mention was made of the contents. Her stepchildren removed everything right after the funeral, including all furnishings, dishes, silverware, washer and dryer, and the refrigerator, as well as the rugs, draperies, and linens. We had to rely on the courts to remedy the situation and prove the husband's intent, but never got back everything.

When there is no surviving spouse or children living in the marital home, several actions should be taken ASAP. Locks to the house/apartment should be changed if no one is living there. No one has a need to access the house except for the person who is in charge of the estate. This is to ensure that personal property items and documents do not go missing.

Second homes or vacation properties should likewise be secured.

Keys to automobiles and recreational equipment should be collected and safeguarded. If the home is vacant, the homeowners insurance company should be notified. If it is an apartment or condo, the property manager should also be notified.

A change of address with the US Postal Service should be filled out so that the mail is sent on to the person in charge.

This is important since sometimes bills and checks arrive only by mail. Monitoring the mail also can reveal other assets owned by the deceased. Forms are available online or at the local post office. If there is a post office box, the keys should be collected.

Locks on storage units should be changed and the manager should be notified so that no one else has access. A rough inventory of the contents should be done.

The police should also be told the house is vacant. Put that notice in writing.

Alarm codes and passwords on home security systems should likewise be changed and the alarm company notified.

All recurring automatic payments should be canceled with all bills rerouted to the person in charge. This would include utilities, Internet, cable TV, cell phones, medical insurance, and any other account. Certain of these, such as cell phone, internet, and cable TV should be disconnected and the service canceled. This also includes medical insurance companies, which should be notified in writing. The insurance company is responsible for all covered medical expenses up until the time of death, even if the billings arrive months later.

CHANGING BENEFICIARY DESIGNATION IF DECEASED WAS NAMED

If the deceased was named as anyone's beneficiary, be sure a new beneficiary is named for wills, trusts, life insurance, investment or deposit accounts, or anything with a beneficiary designation. You may have to redo your own estate planning documents if the deceased was to be a personal representative or trustee. If you were a joint owner of an asset with the deceased, be sure the asset is now legally in your name. If the asset is real estate, file a death certificate with the county deeds office.

CANCELING OR MEMORIALIZING DIGITAL PRESENCE

When a person dies, his or her digital presence may still be around for a long time. Sites like Facebook, Twitter, YouTube,

Instagram, and other social media sites have their own procedures when notified of a member's death. Then there is cloud storage, email, owned websites, virtual currencies, and others that need to be dealt with at death. There is at this time no uniformity in the way death is treated by these site administrators as set out in the terms and conditions fine print. Some will shut down the person's account. Others will allow access to the digital assets if you have the passwords, or upon instruction from a court of law.

Facebook, for example, will allow you to direct what shall happen at the time of your death. You might want the member's page deleted, or have it converted by the person you choose to make it a memorial site. See Appendix M for procedures for Facebook, Instagram, and Twitter.

For other social media accounts, check with the account's website or use a search engine, since new social media accounts are created and become popular on a regular basis. Using the deceased's smartphone will also give you clues as to what apps the person may have been using.

You, as the administrator of the estate, should not ignore the digital presence of the deceased. Identity theft is very common when a person dies, with hackers opening credit card accounts, getting loans in the name of the deceased, and accessing online stores. Virtual currencies, online bank accounts, and other digital assets might be a major part of the assets available for the heirs. If you are lucky, the deceased shared login names and passwords with someone or kept a password ledger. Otherwise, it will likely be time-consuming to pry the needed information from the site administrators, if you can do it at all.

Employers should be told and requested to forward statements on accrued but unpaid wages, bonuses, vacation days, retirement contributions, stock options, and personal property left with the employer.

Financial planners should be contacted since they will have access to some or all investment and insurance accounts and can assist in filing death claims for various benefits.

The Social Security Administration is typically notified of the death by the funeral home. Ask them to verify that. If they did not, the personal representative can make the notification by visiting their local office or by calling the SSA's toll-free number, 800-772-1213. Notice of death to Social Security cannot be made online. Application for survivor benefits is explained in Chapter 12.

If the deceased was self-employed, then business partners, managers, and employees should be notified to facilitate ongoing operation of the business and preserve its value.

All prescription medications should be collected and returned to the pharmacy for disposal. This is especially important for controlled substances such as pain pills. Any medical equipment such as walkers, hospital beds, crutches, and wheelchairs as well as medical supplies can be donated to appropriate agencies. Contact a local health organization or pharmacy, which will see that your donation ends up in the right hands.

MINOR OR DISABLED CHILDREN: CUSTODY, CHILD SUPPORT, GUARDIANSHIP

If the deceased had full custody of minor children and the surviving parent is appropriate for custody, that person is likely already aware of the death and should be able to provide temporary or permanent care for the children. The person in charge should provide access to the home to retrieve clothing and necessary personal items.

If the parent had joint custody, he or she will likely end up with full custody. Remember, though, that custody is a legal term that is under the control and supervision of the court system. Sometimes the noncustodial parent is not a fit parent for full custody or might not be able or willing to fulfill that role. In that case a sibling or grandparent may petition the court for partial or full custody. They can also ask for specific grandparent visitation rights if they do not get custody. A family law attorney can advise as to these rights and procedures.

If the deceased had a written will or guardianship designation appointing who should be the guardian, that person
should be notified immediately unless there is a suitable surviving parent able and willing to take custody. This can be a sticky
situation if the named guardian in a will is not the surviving
parent. A court might have to sort this out.

As to a child support order, if the deceased parent is the
one who was paying child support, the family attorney should
look to see if there was a provision in the divorce judgment for
a guarantee of continued support in the event of the death of
the payer. Sometimes a noncustodial parent will be required to
maintain a life insurance policy or have escrowed funds to continue the support payments after his or her death.

What if the deceased owed a child support arrearage? This
can sometimes amount to thousands of dollars. The arrearage is
likely a valid claim against the deceased's estate. Again, ask the
family law attorney.

If the minor children are the heirs of the estate, then they
will in most cases have to have a court-appointed conservator
to manage their inheritance until they reach the age of majority.
If the deceased had a properly funded trust, then no conservatorship should be necessary since the trust will have already
appointed a trustee to manage the funds. In the case of a modest small inheritance, the state law may allow a surviving parent
to be in charge of the money without a full-blown conservatorship proceeding.

If the deceased is the guardian of disabled children who are
adults and who are the subject of adult guardianship orders due
to either physical or mental disability, they will need to have a
replacement guardian and conservator appointed by the court
in their place for the children. Again, a family law attorney can
assist in this process.

Children who are on financial aid for college may be able
to get help from the college or institution from such things
as a federal Pell Grant. The fact that one or both parents are
deceased means that the application for financial aid needs to

be redone since the financial information on the family is now different. Additionally, there are a number of scholarships available to children of a deceased parent. Go online or ask the college financial aid office. Crowdfunding (such as GoFundMe. com) might also be appropriate.

CHAPTER FOUR

Information Gathering

A major part of the process of winding down the affairs of a deceased's estate is finding and collecting all the information about the deceased's assets and business affairs. If you are lucky enough to be handling the estate of an organized person then there may be files covering all aspects of the person's financial life. Otherwise, here are some things to look for.

ESTATE PLANNING DOCUMENTS

You should look for a last will and testament or a trust document of some kind. If you find a will, be sure you have a signed original. An unsigned will can be useful and could provide evidence of a person's state of mind, but it is not a valid legal document. There may be an exception if the will you find is in the handwriting of the deceased and shows what we call testamentary intent. A handwritten will is called in the law a holographic will.

HANDWRITTEN/HOLOGRAPHIC WILL

State law determines whether a handwritten will is legal. Some states recognize their validity and some do not. States that do recognize them are Alaska, Arizona, Arkansas, California, Colorado, Idaho, Kentucky, Louisiana, Maine, Michigan, Mississippi, Montana, Nebraska, Nevada, New Jersey, North Carolina, North Dakota, Oklahoma, Pennsylvania, South Dakota, Tennessee, Texas, Utah, Virginia, West Virginia, and

Wyoming. A few other states not on this list will recognize one as legal if it has already been admitted to probate in the other state.

But each state has its own requirements as to what parts of the handwritten will must be in the person's writing and whether it needs to be witnessed, notarized, and dated. The validity of such a will is determined by a probate judge after testimony by witnesses. They may testify to their familiarity with the person's handwriting, or if they witnessed it being signed. The testator (will maker) must have intended the writing to be a will, and not just notes that would be later used to make a will. There are exceptions to wills made while in the military in some states. An estate attorney will be able to run down the requirements to prove it a legal will.

The testator must have been mentally competent to make the will. Witnesses can testify to that as well. Holographic wills are often challenged in court. If the will is not allowed, then the testator will either be considered intestate (without a will, so state law would determine who are the legal heirs), or a previous unrevoked will could be considered for admission to probate.

Multiple wills are sometimes presented to courts, leaving a judge with the decision as to which will, if any, is valid. Generally, signing a will automatically revokes all prior wills. So, while the date of a will is considerable evidence, the later will must be shown to have been signed under the correct procedures, while competent, and while not under undue influence or coercion. Those requirements are the basis for will contests.

FINDING THE WILL OR TRUST

If you cannot find a will in a person's effects, ask relatives, financial advisors, and, if the person had one, his or her attorney. Sometimes wills are filed with the court in advance of death for safekeeping. The will is not at that point public record but is kept in a sealed envelope until the court clerk is notified of the person's death. Checking with the courthouse sometimes pays off.

Attorneys in possession of a person's will are required to turn it over to the court clerk, who will notify the named personal representative.

The fact that an attorney prepared a will does not mean that the attorney must be the one who probates the estate, even if the attorney is nominated by the testator in the written document. Choosing and hiring an attorney is the prerogative of the personal representative. Some attorneys keep the original will in what they call their "will safe." On the one hand, this is a way of assuring that the will is not going to be lost. On the other, it is a definite business building tool of a lot of attorneys. The client would have to go back to the lawyer to make any codicils or changes to the will (or trust), and at the time of death the heirs would naturally go to the law office holding the original will. If the attorney is advised of the death of the client, the attorney must first turn the original will over to the local court where the deceased lived. They do not get to begin a probate proceeding unless they are hired to do so by the nominated personal representative of the estate.

Trusts. Like a will, a trust is a written document stating who gets what, when they get it, and who is in charge of seeing that is done. Trusts do not need to be probated, while wills do, and that is one advantage that trusts have over wills. There are lots of kinds of trusts and lots of attorneys who do nothing their entire legal careers except prepare and administer trusts. It used to be that only the wealthy had what was considered a rather exotic estate planning method. Nowadays trusts are a common and accepted way of settling an estate.

Funding. Funding is the process of transferring things into the name of the trust by either putting the asset directly in the name of the trust, or naming the trust as the beneficiary of the asset. If you have minor children you can also use the pour-over will to nominate a guardian for them.

POUR-OVER WILLS

One type of will is also sometimes prepared but we hope not to have to use it. It's called a pour-over will and is a backup way to get assets into the name of the trust in cases where an asset was not funded to the trust prior to death. The idea is that the will "pours over" the non-trust assets to the trust. If the trust was properly funded, there will be no assets left out of the trust and so we will not need the will. Some attorneys do no funding at all before death, relying on the pour-over will to transfer the assets via the probate process. The attorney then gets paid for the probate as well as for the trust.

This plan works, but adds unnecessary expense and time delays to the estate settlement process. The maker of a trust should be sure to transfer newly acquired assets to the trust. It is not unusual to find that even a major asset such as real estate has to be probated because the trust owner did not get around to transferring title into the trust name.

I am not going into great detail about the creation and use of trusts since this is beyond the scope of this book. (It is also covered extensively in *Living Trusts for Everyone*, by me and available from this publisher.)

Finding the signed original trust documents is important. A well-written trust contains directives as to how the trust assets are to be managed as well as who becomes the trustee at the death or disability of the trust maker (usually called the grantor or trustor). That person becomes the successor trustee according to the directives of the document. There may be more than one successor trustee, in which case they will be called co-successor trustees. Or there may be a first successor trustee and then an alternate successor trustee in the event the first successor trustee is unable or unwilling to act as the trustee. There will likely be instructions as to who will be the trustee if none of the named ones are willing or able to be the trustee. Sound confusing? It really isn't. The idea is to be sure all the "what ifs" are covered so that a judge is not needed to appoint a trustee.

Most people store their trust with other important documents like insurance policies, birth certificates, passports, and deeds. When a trust is prepared it is normal procedure and very important to prepare other ancillary documents at the same time. There might be a trust summary, sometimes called a trust certificate, which is usually one or two pages that can be used to open bank or investment accounts.

Additional documents include an assignment of personal property to the trust and a power of attorney to be used by a successor trustee while the grantor is alive, if needed, as well as medical directives to make medical decisions for the grantor if they are unable to make them themselves.

Couples usually create a joint trust that typically names the survivor as the sole trustee and names successor trustees who do not take over until both grantors are deceased or disabled.

LOST DOCUMENTS

If you find documents such as deeds that have been used to transfer title to the trust but cannot find the trust itself, there are some ways to possibly find the original. Check with the attorney who prepared the deed or other documents. (The attorney's name will be on the deed as the preparer.) While it is not typical, some attorneys keep the original trust in their files for safekeeping. If you have notarized documents it might be possible to track down the notary, who may have been working with the attorney. If the lawyer does not have the original but has a photocopy, a judge can have the copy marked as a duplicate original under your state's lost document law. An Affidavit of Lost Document is prepared, signed, and notarized, and a local judge has the authority to declare a true copy as a replacement. This is true in most if not all states. You will likely need a lawyer to take care of this.

Some government agencies, such as a court clerk's office, have provisions where they can accept the trust document or will for safekeeping without actually opening a probate case. The documents are sealed and not public record unless a probate case is opened. This is a long shot, since most people don't do this, but worth a try. Otherwise, if you can't find an original or a signed copy, the estate may have to go through the probate process. Probate isn't the end of the world, but it can be time-consuming and expensive. The fact that the trust cannot be found may create the legal assumption that it was destroyed, and absent any other will the deceased would be declared intestate (without a will) and state law would then determine the next of kin and heirs of the deceased.

CHAPTER FIVE

Identifying Estate Assets

DEPOSIT ACCOUNTS, INVESTMENTS, BROKERAGE

You, as the person in charge of the estate, should have an organized way of storing information on all the various kinds of assets a person could have. Maybe just a set of labeled file folders. When everything is settled you should be prepared to produce an accounting of all the assets you have identified and all the expenditures you have made to settle the estate. This is important to satisfy heirs as well as address any tax issues.

Bank accounts and other similar assets typically produce monthly, quarterly, and annual statements. Print these out if hard copies are not sent. You might need to meet with agents of the institutions (actually or virtually) to prove you have signature authority over the accounts. Each will want at least a copy if not a certified copy of the death certificate.

With checking accounts, you should review the last year's transactions to identify other assets and continuing payments that have been made.

Then check with the institutions to see if the deceased named a beneficiary or joint owner for the account. Not everyone knows that beneficiaries can be named on these types of assets. If a beneficiary or a joint owner is named, your job is to just notify them of that fact and they can then make their own arrangements to collect the funds. If the beneficiary is the deceased's trust, then the trustee will make the claim and the asset will be turned over to the trustee. If there is no beneficiary named and the account is not in the name of the trust or a joint owner, then a probate procedure of some type (expedited or regular process) will have to be used to collect the assets.

PASSWORDS TO ONLINE ACCOUNTS, COMPUTERS, SMARTPHONES

You should try to access cell phones, computers, tablets, and online sites saved as favorites of the deceased. That means you need their usernames and passwords. Most people have made a list of them just to remind themselves of these. Passwords should be changed occasionally, so it is likely there is a list somewhere of the current ones. If you can get into the person's computer, autofill might complete the password for you. Otherwise, it will be very difficult if not impossible to get this information. One of the very important things we need in estate settlement is access to the online asset accounts, such as banking and brokerage accounts. If you do not have the passwords for these you will have to contact the institution directly and provide proof that the person is deceased and that you are the one in charge. The death certificate and either the Letters of Authority from the probate court or an Affidavit of Trust should be enough proof to convince the institution to give you access to the accounts.

Microsoft is generally not helpful in retrieving passwords from the computer of the deceased. You can spend hours online trying to get help, but there is a simpler way. A data recovery computer company can likely gain access to the files on the computer provided that the data has not been encrypted. Now, technology changes fast, so any advice I give is likely to be outdated by the time this book is printed and you read it, but using computer consultants is probably your best bet if you can't get the information you need with a court order.

SAFE-DEPOSIT BOX

Accessing a safe-deposit box can be very simple if the deceased listed you as an authorized person and gave you a key. Simply

show up, sign in, and you will be allowed to view the box contents privately. You can even remove all of the contents and take
them with you.

If you are not a listed signatory on the box, it is a bit more
difficult. Bank procedures vary, but generally you will need to
fill out paperwork at the probate court, then make an appointment with the city or county treasurer who will meet you at the
bank or depository and inventory the contents of the box. This
is to be sure that the contents and their value are reported to the
court and listed on a probate inventory if probate is required.
This also ensures that the authorities will get the taxes on the
found assets. If there is a last will and testament in the box, it
must be turned over to the probate court. Some states require
you to provide the death certificate and photo identification
and that the bank photocopy and inventory the contents. Look
to state and local laws for the procedure or just ask someone at
the bank what they require.

People will often store insurance policies, bonds, jewelry,
and other things of interest to the estate, so getting into the box
can be quite important. Be prepared to provide family members
and listed heirs with a copy of the inventory to allay any suspi-
cion that you have not given them full disclosure.

STORAGE LOCKERS

As stated previously, getting the keys to a storage unit should
be one of the priorities on your to-do list. Inventorying the
contents and changing the lock will ensure that no one else
will be removing items. You should be sure to contact the management and arrange to keep the rental paid on it until you
can dispose of the items. Go over the check register and credit
card statements to possibly identify the locker company if you
suspect there was a locker but don't know which company was
renting out the unit.

In one estate I handled there was evidence that the deceased
owned a collectible car—one of those 1960s "muscle" cars of
high value—but we did not know where it was located. No

one in the family knew. But we had the title and registration, so we knew it had not been sold. The location was finally discovered after we found automatic monthly payments to a company from the deceased's MasterCard account. The name on the credit card statement didn't indicate it was a storage unit, but when I tracked it down and produced the death certificate and court-ordered Letters of Authority, they cut the lock off for me and there it was. So, investigate.

INSURANCE POLICIES

One of the big items to be found in an asset search is a life insurance policy. There is always a hard copy, and these are usually found in a safe-deposit box or in with the deceased's other important papers. And there might be more than one. As we know, these typically have named beneficiaries on them and their names are listed on the insurance contract. To collect on them, the beneficiary will fill out a claim form, available from the insurance company, and send it in with a copy of the death certificate. If the beneficiaries are adults and if the company does not dispute the claim, the policy proceeds are usually paid within thirty days.

Insurance companies don't build those big office towers by paying out claims willy-nilly. They can deny a claim based on fraud or if they can prove suicide. In most states there is an incontestability law that states that suicide can be raised as a defense against nonpayment of a claim only if the suicide occurred within the first two years of the policy issuance. Fraud is usually asserted if the insured lied about his or her medical history; for example, failing to reveal a known serious medical condition when asked on an insurance application.

Life insurance policies are also provided by employers, fraternal organizations, sometimes credit card companies, and even automobile finance companies (so-called credit life policies that pay off the balance owed on an auto loan). In the next chapter I will discuss how to find out whether there was other unknown life insurance coverage on the deceased's life.

Other insurance contracts may come into play. In a case I had, the deceased died in a house fire and the insurance company refused to pay for the loss of the house and contents, claiming that there was evidence of arson. We had to hire our own investigators to show that the cause of the fire was just as likely an accident in order to get them to pay.

Annuities are insurance contracts and may also have a death benefit depending on the type of annuity and how long it has been in existence.

If the deceased had a reverse mortgage on their house, then this might also have a death benefit, depending upon how much equity exists over the balance of the mortgage.

SELF-EMPLOYED AND SMALL-BUSINESS OWNERS

Assets owned by the self-employed are usually more than just a bank account and office furniture. There may be accounts receivable, inventory, intellectual property such as patents, contracts for ongoing work, royalty rights, oil, gas, and mineral leases—and lots of other things.

If the business is a brick-and-mortar store, or an office space, you must secure the sites and communicate with any employees. A manager employee might be able to continue the business for a time if the ongoing business has transferable value. Control of the business cash and banking accounts and an inventory of product would be called for. There might be family members or a working partner who can continue the business operation.

If it is a partnership, LLC, or small corporation you need to see if there is a partnership or buyout agreement. Very often partners will take out life insurance policies on each other to provide funds to buy out the interests of the deceased partner's family. If there was none, then a business valuation appraisal will have to be done to determine the value of the deceased's share.

There might be significant digital assets attributable to online activities such as web-based stores, affiliate programs, PayPal, eBay, and online bank and gambling accounts. Credit card processors will transfer funds directly to the business owner's account. Online savings accounts are now popular and offer paperless statements. All these things should be looked for and the passwords discovered.

ACCOUNTING SERVICES

Most small businesses use accounting services. The business accountant can readily identify sources of income and approximate depreciated values of business assets. They can also provide copies of business and personal tax returns, which often contain clues as to other assets. They are the appropriate ones to call to prepare the year-of-death business and personal tax returns.

EMPLOYMENT BENEFITS, STOCK OPTIONS, UNION BENEFITS

There can be a wide variety of employment-related benefits—or none at all. Types of benefits include disability insurance, health insurance, dental, vision, legal, paid vacation, maternity, child care, and club and gym memberships. Money-related benefits include retirement plans including pensions, 401(k)s, deferred compensation, stock options, life insurance, the last paycheck, and accrued bonuses—I am sure there are others. For purposes of estates the only things we are interested in are those that result in an ultimate benefit for heirs.

These accounts generally allow beneficiary designations, but that doesn't mean that the deferred income tax has to be paid by the beneficiary immediately. This is another area where you will want assistance from your tax professional. In Appendix I I have included verbatim information from the Internal Revenue Service that thoroughly covers the topic of rollovers. The plan of many beneficiaries is to add the amount of the deceased's 401(k) or IRA to their own IRA to increase their retirement fund while continuing to defer the income tax on the deferred compensation.

Keep in mind though that when you retire, there comes a time when you must start taking money out of the retirement accounts. These are called required minimum distributions. The IRS doesn't want to wait forever to collect those deferred taxes.

Sometimes these plans will allow the spouse and children of an employee to continue receiving some of the benefits after the death of the employee. Medical insurance comes to mind. Others are accrued but not received benefits, such as unused vacation days, the value from which sometimes go to heirs. Of course, the money ones are of most importance to you as the one gathering assets for the estate.

The deceased's human resources office can give you forms and applications for the turnover of all accrued employee benefits in most cases. If the employee was a member of a labor union, the union representative can provide similar help. Employee handbooks usually list the items to which the employee was entitled.

If there is a surviving spouse, some of these may be able to carry over in full or in part at no cost or modest cost. Some of the benefits could have beneficiaries named, but you will want to apprise them of that benefit and claim procedure so that they may file the proper claim.

TAX RETURNS

Two things are relevant here. Identifying assets revealed by the income tax returns, and filing status.

The rule on filing status is that a surviving spouse can file as married filing jointly for the year of death, but not thereafter. This option usually results in a lower tax liability.

If the surviving spouse has a qualifying dependent child (as defined in IRS rules, which can include not just the spouse's children but also stepchildren and adopted children but not foster children), then they may file for years two and three as a qualifying widow(er). This entitles a surviving spouse with child(ren) to take additional standard deduction amounts similar to the amounts available to a married couple filing jointly.

There are rules as to whether you qualify for this additional deduction. First, it is not available if you remarry. Second, the qualifying child must have lived with you for the year you are claiming that filling status. Third, you must have paid at more than half of the expenses of the home you and the child are living in. This includes all living expenses including rent or mortgage, utilities, taxes, and food.

The big caveat is to talk to a tax professional to determine your proper IRS filing status. And remember that state and city income tax rules might be different than the federal ones. The information in this book is not intended to be legal, financial, or tax advice, even though we believe it to be true at the time this book was written. Tax laws change all the time, so get current tax advice before filing.

ACCOUNTS RECEIVABLE, LAND CONTRACTS, PERSONAL LOANS

Accounts receivable sounds like something only businesses deal with. But there are times when you are owed money by others. One of the most common is when you sell real estate on monthly payments instead of for cash. Whether it's called a Land Contract or a Contract for Deed, the idea is that you, as the seller, are acting as a mortgage company for the buyer. When the buyer finishes paying off the contract, you convey the legal ownership with a warranty deed.

Sometimes the contract is for a set length of time at the expiration of which the balance on the contract must be paid in full. This is called a balloon payment. You can download mortgage amortization schedules to see how much of the monthly payment goes toward interest and how much is applied to the principal of the contract.

If the deceased had sold property using this financing device, the contract is an asset of the estate. The death of the seller does not affect the rights of the buyer, who will continue making the payments, but the payments would then be paid either to the person to whom the contract was assigned after probate or to the deceased's trust, if there was no probate and the seller had placed the contract into the name of the trust.

If there is more than one heir, one or more of the heirs may agree to accept the contract rights as part of their share of the estate, or the payments can be divided pro rata according to the respective share of the estate, or the contract may be sold for its discounted present value and the proceeds of the sale divided.

LOANS MADE TO CHILDREN AND OTHER HEIRS

What if there were loans made by the deceased to heirs? It is not uncommon for parents to lend their children money, and sometimes they actually are paying it back—and it might even be evidenced by a written promissory note. Often there is no written agreement or formal loan document, but there might be letters or emails that can support whether it was intended as a gift or as a loan. This can be a sticky subject among siblings. The borrower may consider the loan a gift with no legal obligation to repay it. This can turn into a legal matter with a judge needed to determine if the loan was in fact a loan and whether it is enforceable as a loan if there was no writing to memorialize it.

One way of handling it is to have the loan amount added to the total estate and then have the amount of the loan deducted from the share of the debtor. If the deceased got good advice he or she would have included in the will or trust an acknowledgement of the loan and set out written instructions to either forgive the debt or describe how that loan should be handled in the ultimate distribution of the estate. Otherwise, the personal representative or trustee could try to get the debtor to validate the legality of the debt. Discuss this with an attorney since there are ways to make a questionably legal debt into a rock-solid enforceable one.

There might be other monies owed to the deceased. Buyout agreements on businesses, farmland, mining, mineral and timber leases, oil and gas leases—all of these would have to be either liquidated or arrangements made for the payments to be sent to the estate. While unusual, there may be lottery winnings that are being paid in installments by the state that would then be claimed by the heirs according to the state lottery rules.

PRENUPTIAL AGREEMENTS

The provisions of a prenuptial (premarital) agreement almost always address the rights of both parties to the marriage if one or both of them should die. Review the agreement with your attorney to see whether the rights of a surviving spouse are in line with the agreement or to determine whether the agreement is even valid. There are numerous grounds for voiding a prenup, including the failure of the parties to fully disclose their assets or liabilities, or insisting on the agreement on the eve of the wedding to force a signature.

DIVORCE DECREES, QUALIFIED DOMESTIC RELATIONS ORDER (QDRO) PROPERTY DIVISION

The final divorce judgment of the deceased contains information you should review even if it is years old and even if there has been a remarriage. The sections on child custody, child support, spousal support (alimony), and property division can all impact the surviving ex-spouse. Sometimes the division of marital assets is not completed at the time of death. This may add assets or liabilities to the estate. One of the most important provisions is the Qualified Domestic Relations Order (QDRO) section, since this sets out the rights of each party in the retirement plan of the other. This order is sent to the retirement plan's administrator who, along with the divorce judge, approves the order and requires the plan to pay a portion of the plan value to the other spouse. Calculations are done at the time of the divorce to fix what will be the dollar amount, which is then collectible at the time of retirement. Typically, the parties then change the beneficiaries of their separate accounts for their separate shares of the retirement account. A prenup can address the retirement asset so that a QDRO is not applicable. This is a specialized legal area and different types of retirement plans are treated differently.

ALIMONY

State law and the divorce decree determine the fate of alimony either received by or owed by a deceased. Generally, the payments stop at the death of either party. Sometimes alimony is tied to a life insurance policy or trust funds that would allow payments to be continued if the payor dies. Absent a specific provision regarding the death of the payor, state laws can control whether payments cease at death or not. For example, Florida has a specific statute that bars alimony after death, but provisions can be made in the divorce judgment to secure continuing payments.

But what about arrearages in alimony? If the payor has not kept up the payments and dies, the amount of the arrearage is a claim against the estate of the payer and the payer's assets including a 401(k) can be used to cover the arrearage.

CHAPTER SIX

How Is a Small Estate Settled?

SMALL ESTATES

Assuming the deceased did not have a trust, the method of collecting and distributing the assets of the estate depend upon two factors: the size of the estate and the makeup of the assets.

Most state laws have special expedited legal processes for small estates. *Small* is a relative word since the expedited methods are available for estates less than $15,000 in Michigan to less than $166,250 in California. This is the amount determined after the deduction of funeral and burial costs, and there might be other credits if there is a surviving spouse. You may use a court-approved affidavit to show you are entitled to use the small estate procedure. Pay a small fee and you will be issued paperwork to show to the institution holding the asset and they will turn it over to the proper heirs.

NON-PROBATE ASSETS

Certain assets are not counted toward the probate exclusion. Jointly owned assets, those with a beneficiary designation or a pay-on-death designation, and assets in the name of a trust are non-probate assets, so even large estates can sometimes use the affidavit procedure to settle the estate by excluding non-probate assets. Attorney advice is recommended, but having read this book you will be speaking to the lawyer with a base of knowledge and so will know the right questions to ask.

TITLED VEHICLES, BOATS, MANUFACTURED HOMES, TRAILERS

Some states have special procedures to transfer title to vehicles, boats, manufactured homes, and trailers, provided there is no ongoing probate case. If there is ongoing probate for other assets, then the simplified transfer procedures cannot be used. However, look at the title document to see who is listed as the owner. Some states allow you to own it in an and/or fashion. For example; John Jones or Mary Jones. This type of ownership means that either John or Mary can sign to transfer the title and both signatures are not needed. John Jones and Mary Jones JWROS (joint with right of survivorship) means that if one of them dies, the survivor is the sole owner of the vehicle/boat/manufactured home/trailer. The survivor can then get a new title in his or her name.

If the title says only John Jones, then in some states the deceased's next of kin can have the title transferred to them through the state motor vehicle bureau provided that there is no probate and the value of the vehicles is less than the state maximum value for the process. In Michigan the total value of the vehicles would have to be less than $60,000 to use this procedure.

A form from the title office that might be called "Certification from the Heir to a Vehicle" will need to be filed to transfer the title. This form, or one like it, can be presented along with a death certificate to transfer title to a surviving spouse or next of kin. If there is no surviving spouse and multiple next of kin, such as three siblings, then the title can be put in all three names, or, if some someone does not want their name on the title, they can sign a certification declining any interest in the vehicle.

The best advice is to check with your local vehicle registration office either online or in person for your local state procedure.

If the transfer of title by certificate does not apply, then the titled assets must be listed as part of the gross probate inventory of assets and the transfer of title would be done by the court appointed personal representative.

You cannot legally sign the name of the deceased on the title to try to slip around the mandated transfer process. And if the deceased had already signed the seller's portion of the title, you have to treat it as if it had not been signed at all. I have seen people do this and not tell the buyer that the seller is dead, but do not recommend it even though they do sometimes get away with it in states where the seller's signature does not have to be notarized.

Manufactured homes are a bit different in the transfer process. If a title to the home was actually issued, and the home was then placed on a permanent foundation, it becomes part of the real estate and the title in most cases will not have to be transferred. When the real estate is sold the manufactured home (which is no longer mobile) is part of the sale of the property. But if the home is placed in a manufactured home park on a rented space, the title transfer process would be the same as for a car. Each state has its own rules and paperwork requirements, so check with them. You might need to provide a bill of sale or other documents.

LIENS ON TITLES

If there is money owed on the titled asset then typically the name of the lender is listed on the title document and before the item can be sold a written statement must be signed by them to release the lien. This statement is usually printed on the title but a separate form from the lender can also be used. Releasing the lien requires paying off the balance on the loan since the titled asset was collateral for the loan.

FINDING LOST ASSETS

Life Insurance. How do we know whether a person had life insurance if we cannot find a policy or certificate proving its existence? Sometimes the policy is paid up, meaning no further premiums ever need to be paid, or it was an employer fringe benefit where there was no policy as such since it was part of a group life policy on all the employees of a firm. An unclaimed insurance policy eventually goes to the government. So how do we know for sure if the deceased was insured? Check all the likely places for a printed policy and also the unlikely places. I had one estate where I had previously interviewed the about-to-be deceased person to be sure her affairs were in order. After her death, during a clean-up of the house prior to its sale, we found an envelope stuck in among some books on a shelf in the kitchen. In it was a paid-up life policy worth $250,000 that she had never mentioned and that the family did not know existed.

If you are a fan of murder mysteries it seems one of the first things the detectives do is try to ascertain who had the most to benefit by the victim's death. They seem to know right away how much insurance was out there and who are the beneficiaries. Well, you can use the same resources as the detectives.

Several states offer free life insurance policy locator services. You need the information from the death certificate to fill out the online forms. They can find only life and annuity policies that were sold in their state and take a while to get back to you, but it's worth a look. Search for "Life Insurance Locator Service." In addition to the state-specific search services there is a nationwide one. The National Association of Insurance Commissioners (NAIC) offers a national service (NAIC.org) that has contacts with most of the life insurance companies. If you provide the information, they will notify all the companies who will then respond directly to you if they have issued such a policy. Be prepared to wait for up to ninety days and they will not contact you if they are unsuccessful.

Unclaimed Bank Accounts. It's not unusual for a deceased person to have told their relatives that there is a bank account with their names on it. It's also not unusual for the heirs to be unable to locate any such account. You can check with banks the deceased used or even those close to their residence. It could be that the account was closed long ago or that someone else had already liquidated the account. If you are certain the account existed, you have the right as the personal representative of the estate to get a record of deposits and withdrawals from the account and even copies of checks written on it if it was a checking account. Using this method, in one case the heirs discovered that a neighbor had been "helping" the deceased with bill paying and had taken over $60,000 from the account. The police got involved on that one, but the money was never recovered.

Every state has an unclaimed property division, which can sometimes locate not only insurance policies but also bank accounts that have had no activity on them for a stated length of time. Typically, there is a search link that will produce a list of all unclaimed accounts. These may also include deposits on utilities, cable and telephone service, rental space, stock dividends, and even unclaimed safe deposit contents. It only takes a minute to search, and if you find something there is a claim procedure to collect the asset through the state. There are services that will look for unclaimed property for a fee. I can't say that they do anything more than use the unclaimed property sites for the states the deceased lived in, so research carefully before you pay a fee for something you could have easily done yourself. Often the unclaimed property turns out to be so small as to hardly be worth pursuing, but you never know.

CHAPTER SEVEN

Debts Owed by the Deceased

When a person dies, do their debts die with them? Sometimes they do. One of the jobs of the person winding up the affairs of the deceased is to find out what debts were owed and the nature of those debts. Whether they are still owed depends on several factors. A further responsibility is to ascertain whether a debt is legitimate or is barred because of some other factor, such as the statute of limitations.

NOTIFY ALL KNOWN CREDITORS, PUBLICATION OF NOTICE, TRUSTS, AND PROBATE

Was the claim for a debt owed by the estate filed too late after notice of publication even though it was otherwise enforceable and valid?

The personal representative or the successor trustee may be required to notify all known creditors of the deceased and provide the time limit for the creditor to file the alleged claim against the estate. The notice is also published in a local newspaper or the appropriate place for legal notices to be published. The time limit is statutory and becomes in effect a shortened statute of limitations. Claims filed after the published date are unenforceable and notice of denial is sent to them.

If a filed claim seems to be illegitimate then the personal representative or trustee can deny the claim in writing and the claimant will have to prove its validity to a court before it will be paid. If they fail to enforce the claim in the appropriate time, then it is barred.

If the claim is the subject of a lawsuit that is ongoing, then the personal representative or trustee can substitute for the deceased to continue to contest the validity of the claim. Any insurance company which was assisting in denying the claim in court will assist the estate in this process. Do not pay a debt just because it seems valid until you are sure you have identified the total liability of the estate for claims. Sometimes there are not enough assets to pay everyone, so they have to take a percentage. You do not want to favor early claimants since you might be personally responsible to the ones who got less than their claim.

JOINT DEBTS, COSIGNERS

Was this a joint debt?
Joint debts are those where the decedent and another person signed the contract. They are what the law calls jointly and severally liable for the debt. On default the creditor can pursue one or both of the joint debtors. This means that the estate may have no responsibility for the debt, although the joint debtor might file a claim against the estate for payment of one-half of the debt.

Was there a cosigner?
A cosigner is similar to a joint debtor loan except the person cosigning is only asked to pay the debt if the original debtor defaults. Cosigners are typically used when the primary debtor has no credit rating or a poor one. If the deceased was the primary debtor, then the cosigner can pay the debt and then file a claim with the estate to recover the payment. If the cosigner was the deceased, then the primary debtor is responsible for the debt.

Was there collateral put up for a loan?
When money is borrowed, sometimes the lender requires that an asset be put up as security for the loan. If the loan is not paid

the borrower may have to surrender the secured property. So, the lender has a secured interest in the property. This is true of automobile sales, for example, where there is a down payment and then monthly payments until the car is paid for or sold. In an estate situation the personal representative may offer to give up the collateral voluntarily if there is little or no equity in it or may sell the collateral and pay off the loan, keeping any surplus for the estate. Family members or heirs cannot just continue making the payments and hold on to the vehicle.

Are there any others who could be responsible for the debt who are not cosigners or co-debtors?

In the case of credit cards, an authorized signer who is not an owner of the credit card account can be held liable for the entire balance on the account if they continue using it after the owner's death. That is why the recommendation is to notify all credit card companies and credit bureaus of the death immediately. An authorized signer's authority to sign ends at the death of the owner and the signer has no responsibility to pay the credit card balance.

Are there other defenses to the claim?
Do you have to pay?

Just because someone files a claim with the court for an alleged debt owed by the deceased does not mean the debt is valid. The trustee or personal representative should ask for documentation proving the claim and if not satisfied should send a notice of disallowance to the claimant. It is then up to them to ask for a court to determine its validity.

TAX CLAIMS, COURT-ORDERED FINES, AND RESTITUTION

What about money owed to the government?

Federally insured student loans are extinguished at the death of the person owing them. The exception is that if you live in a community property state and your spouse dies, you could be responsible for paying their student loans depending upon the type of student loan and depending upon state law. Private nongovernmental student loans are often cosigned, but otherwise it is likely, again depending on state law and the loan contract, that the debt is extinguished with death. Again, check with your attorney to be certain of the current law. These things change all the time.

Claims for court-ordered fines and restitution for criminal cases may be enforceable depending upon the state law. The person owed the restitution would have to file a claim and prove the balance owed before it is required to be paid. Money owed to the IRS can also be a claim against the estate, which claim can be contested by the personal representative if appropriate. Sometimes the estate will make an offer of settlement to pay less than the amount demanded in order to expedite the closing of the claim.

Income or other tax claims have priority over general unsecured claims. If the taxes are in dispute, the trustee or personal representative takes over in objecting to the tax claim and can sometimes resolve it for less than is being claimed.

MORTGAGES

A mortgage is another example of a secured debt. If the mortgage is not paid then it can be foreclosed and the house sold by the lender to pay the mortgage debt. If there is a surplus, which is not typical, then that is paid to the borrower or the estate of a deceased borrower. Sometimes there is more than one borrower, and if the co-borrower continues to make the payments then there is no foreclosure. The problems come when someone who is not a co-owner of the property and whose name is not on the mortgage wants to continue to live in the house and wants to continue making the payments.

Most mortgages have a provision that accelerates the entire mortgage balance if there are no living listed borrowers. The people who want to stay in the house would have to do one of two things. First is to get the agreement from the estate to buy the house, and second, to apply for and get a mortgage of their own to facilitate the sale if they are unable to pay cash and satisfy the mortgage. They cannot just continue paying the mortgage payments. If the house has been left specifically to a particular person, the mortgage still must be paid in full by that person or the estate before the house can be given to them. Look for language in the will or trust that might specify whether the property is to be given to the heir free of debt.

If there are enough assets in the estate, and the person who wants the house has an inheritance big enough to cover the mortgage, then the personal representative can pay the mortgage using the share of that person and then deed it over to them free and clear.

What if the personal representative wants to sell the house with the new buyer assuming the mortgage and taking over the payments? Once upon a time that could be done, but nowadays nearly all mortgages have what they call a due-on-sale clause that accelerates the balance due so that no mortgage assumptions are possible.

LAND CONTRACTS/CONTRACTS FOR DEED

Land contracts, also called contracts for deed, may be another matter. These are contracts between a buyer and seller where the seller acts like a bank and receives a down payment and monthly payments for a set number of years. These can be assumable or assignable if the contract provisions allow it. The initial buyer or the estate of the initial buyer will likely not be released from liability and acts like a cosigner to pay the contract off if the assignee fails to make the payments.

REVERSE MORTGAGES

A reverse mortgage is like a mortgage where the property owner borrows the money based on a percentage of the equity in the property. But they do not pay it back so long as they live in the house as their primary residence and continue paying taxes, insurance, utilities, and maintenance on the property. The lender charges interest on the loan amount, which is added every month to the mortgage balance. The property owner can stay in the house for life, regardless of the mortgage balance. Then at the time the owner dies the house is sold, the mortgage is paid off, and any remaining sale proceeds go to the estate of the owner. It is important to know all the costs and fees involved in a reverse mortgage. The interest rate is important to keep the monthly interest charges as low as possible.

Sometimes the borrower elects to take monthly payments from the lender rather than a lump sum. Or they may agree to have a line of credit from the lender, which can be drawn on as needed. Those withdrawals are added to the principal amount of the mortgage. The interest added to the mortgage, then is based on the mortgage principal plus accrued interest on the loan.

There are lots of law provisions regulating reverse mortgages designed to forestall past abuses of these contracts. To qualify for this type of mortgage the borrowers have to be at least sixty-two years of age. So, if one partner is seventy and the other is sixty, then only the seventy-year-old can be on the contract. At that person's death (or if they no longer use the home as their primary residence—like if they are in a nursing home) the contract comes due and the survivor will have to refinance if possible or otherwise pay off the mortgage debt, which will be much more than the amount borrowed. There may be no equity left for the survivor, who also now has no place to live.

This is a complicated type of mortgage, and if your deceased had one of these you will need to work with a real estate attorney to be sure that the mortgage was valid under the law and to be sure the payoff amount is correct.

LEASES AS LANDLORD OR TENANT

A real estate lease, whether on a house or apartment, is a contract. As such, the contract language, along with the statutory law, spells out the rights and duties of both the landlord and the tenant. You pay the rent, you can stay. Don't pay the rent, you get evicted. There are other rights and duties of course, but for our purposes we need to look at the lease to answer several questions.

If the deceased was the landlord, the estate steps into that role and collects the rent and maintains the property according to the terms of the lease, which do not change at the death of the landlord. The estate eventually either sells the property subject to the lease, or transfers the property to the heirs—again, subject to the lease.

If the tenant died and there were furnishings and personal property left in the unit, then state law may determine the rights of the landlord in clearing out the property in order to offer it for rent. It is the duty of the landlord to safeguard the property, so you should photograph the interior, change the locks, give a key to the personal representative of the deceased, and not let anyone into the property or remove items unless accompanied by you.

If someone else is living in the property who is not on the lease, then you should either have them sign a new lease or give them notice to quit possession of the property according to the landlord/tenant laws.

If the deceased was the tenant, then we need to know if the lease agreement says anything about the tenant's death. Was the lease for a set period of time or was it a month-to-month rental? If it was for a stated period of time, such as one year, then the landlord can enforce the terms of the lease requiring monthly payments until the end of the lease contract. Local laws may require the landlord to try to lease the property to someone else during that time to ameliorate the loss to the estate.

Security deposits are an asset of the estate, but the landlord retains the right to assess the estate for damages to the property to be deducted from the deposit. The estate retains rights under state or local law to contest these charges. A real estate attorney can tell you how this is handled by law in the locality of the rental unit. Any remainder of the deposit becomes an estate asset.

You may, in most cases, apply the security deposit to unpaid rent. If there is still rent due for the term of the lease after all credits are applied, you may file a claim with the personal representative or trustee. But see the section below on insolvent estates.

VEHICLE LEASES

Automobile or truck leases usually do not expire at the death of the lessee. Read the lease contract carefully. Sometimes the lessor will agree to terminate the contract and take possession of the vehicle. Barring that, the estate will be responsible for paying the lease payments. If there was a cosigner on the lease, that person is responsible for continuing the payments. It is possible there is an early termination provision in the lease contract dealing with death, but that is unlikely. The local dealer may in fact want to allow the lease to be terminated, but they might not have the legal authority to do so. Most lease contracts are not carried by the dealer but are sold or assigned to a third-party leasing company, which is less likely than the dealer to try to help out the family of the deceased.

CREDIT CARDS

When one dies and has credit card debt, does it have to be paid? Sometimes no. It depends on a number of things, including the state the person resided in at death and whether there were any co-owners of the credit card account. If there was a co-owner, then the death of one of the owners does not let the other off the hook for paying the debt. A co-owner is one who actually signed the application for the credit card. This is different from an authorized user.

AUTHORIZED USERS OF CREDIT CARDS

An authorized user has no responsibility for paying the credit card debt. Normally, you can tell who is the owner of the card account by looking at the billing statement. If you are an authorized user, then in most cases your name will not be listed on the billing. However, if you continue to use the card after the owner's death, you can be held responsible and possibly even criminally responsible for fraudulent use.

In community property states (Alaska, Arizona, California, Idaho, Louisiana, Nevada, New Mexico, Texas, Washington, or Wisconsin), a spouse can be held responsible for the credit card debt of their deceased partner even if they were not a co-owner of the card because those states treat a spouse as a legal co-owner of the account even if they never used it themselves.

It might be possible to have the survivor take over the account and continue to use it if the card issuer is willing to rely on the credit worthiness of the survivor, but this is a long shot. In the terms and conditions fine print on the card application most all companies say the card is canceled on death. The entire balance is then due as a debt of the estate.

Some cards offer reward programs such as frequent flyer miles based on usage of the card. At the death of the card owner most cards do not allow the accrued miles to go with the estate or to heirs. I was told that if you have the password to the frequent flyer program you can successfully book trips using the miles even after the person's death. I believe that is fraud and should not be done. Just because people do it doesn't make it legal.

The personal representative or trustee should report the death to all three major credit reporting agencies. This will ensure that no one can apply for credit in the name of the deceased. Identity theft can create problems for the estate. Here are what I believe to be current contact information for them:

Experian, 888-397-3742, P.O. Box 9701, Allen, Texas 75013. https://www.experian.com/contact/personal-services-contacts.html

Equifax, 800-525-6285, P.O. Box 105069, Atlanta, Georgia 30348. https://www.equifax.com/personal/

TransUnion, 800-680-7289, P.O. Box 6790, Fullerton, California 92834. https://www.transunion.com/customer-support /login/4

CHAPTER EIGHT

Paying Debts, Distributing Assets to Heirs

Settling an estate is done in three steps. Identify the assets, identify legitimate debts and expenses, and distribute the remainder to the heirs. Sounds simple, but if you are not careful some creditors may end up favored over others, leaving less for the heirs.

Paying debts and expenses too soon is a common mistake made by trustees and personal representatives. What you don't want to do is to start paying the debts of the deceased as soon as they are presented to you. Since we don't know the ultimate total of debts, it sometimes happens that the creditors who turn in their debts early are preferred over those sending them in later on. The reason this can happen is because sometimes the final total of assets available to distribute to creditors is less than the amount of total presented and legitimate debt. The normal process is to wait to pay anyone until we know those two final totals. If there is more debt than there are distributable assets, the creditors will have to take cents-on-the-dollar so that all creditors are treated equally pro rata. This segues to the next topic.

THE INSOLVENT ESTATE

Insolvent just means that the total of the allowable claims in an estate (I like to call it the debt) exceeds the usable assets. If that's the case then the creditors only get a portion, or none, of their claim. It's not just the creditors who get a piece of the asset pie. Certain expenses have priority over money paid to creditors. In other words, the creditors are last in line to be paid what the deceased owed.

Sometimes we don't know the estate is insolvent until after the time limit is up for creditors to file claims against the estate. The personal representative is required to notify all known creditors and to publish a notice to unknown creditors letting all know that the person has died, who is the personal representative, and the procedure and time limit for filing any claims for debts owed by the deceased. The time limit is statutory so it may vary from state to state. But it creates a shorter statute of limitations than would apply if the deceased hadn't died. Any claims filed after that date are barred. So, if the claims exceed the assets available after deduction of priority items, then the estate is insolvent.

PRIORITY OF CLAIMS: WHO GETS PAID FIRST

Here is the list of priority claims in Michigan, which is pretty much the same as most other states, with my explanation of what they are:

(a) Costs and expenses of administration. This includes attorney fees, court filing fees, inventory fees, legal advertising, court-appointed guardian ad litem fees, personal representative fees. This in effect is a type of tax as far as the estate is concerned. The court system and attorney fees are a priority over any assets going to the family of the deceased.

(b) Reasonable funeral and burial expenses. Self-explanatory.

(c) If the deceased was survived by a spouse or minor children or both, and there were assets in the individual name of the deceased (not held jointly with the spouse) and those separate assets required probate, then the surviving spouse or minor children, or both, are entitled to the following distributions from the estate in addition to any other distribution to which they may have been entitled by will or intestacy. (Wow, that was a long sentence.) These entitlements are superior to claims of creditors. So, the surviving family gets additional assets from the estate even if creditors get only a portion of their claim. As a practical matter these rarely are a consideration since most often assets are held jointly with the surviving spouse, or the surviving spouse and children are beneficiaries of the deceased, so there is no probate needed for the deceased.

(d) Homestead allowance. This is a payment to the surviving spouse and minor children paid after the above priority claims but before any payment to creditors. The amount is fixed by state law.

(e) Family allowance. Another payment to spouse and children but is paid monthly or otherwise during the pendency of probate.

(f) Exempt property. Some assets are exempt from claims of creditors. These include household furnishings, appliances, cars (one or more depending on the state but not to include cars that are collateral for a loan), and personal effects.

(g) Debts and taxes with priority under federal law, including, but not limited to, medical assistance payments that are subject to adjustment or recovery from an estate under section 1917 of the Social Security Act, 42 USC 1396. These are liens that can be placed against an estate for Medicaid reimbursement in certain cases.

(h) Reasonable and necessary medical and hospital expenses of the deceased's last illness, including a compensation of persons attending the deceased.

(i) Debts and taxes with priority under other laws of this state. Can include past due child support or spousal support, tax arrearages, student loans, court-ordered fines, or reparations.

(j)   All other claims. Here is where the credit cards and other personal debts are paid pro rata. If they are all paid in full, the rest goes to the heirs.

The examples of priority claims listed are a way of ensuring that a surviving spouse and minor children are provided with living expenses and assets during the pendency of probate. In effect, general unsecured creditors might be having their claims reduced by the entitlements of the priority claims. For the surviving family that is a good thing. Having the homestead and family allowance provides for the surviving family even if the estate is otherwise insolvent.

An estate is therefore insolvent if after payment of all priority claims there is not enough left in the estate to pay the creditors in full. The probate process must still be completed with partial or no payment to creditors and the estate then closed.

If there were no assets solely in the name of the deceased, then no probate of any kind is needed. The surviving spouse takes all jointly owned assets as well as all assets on which the survivor is the beneficiary. Joint debts continue to be paid by the survivor, but debts solely in the name of the deceased do not have to be paid. If you receive billings for these, send a letter along with a copy of the death certificate to the company sending the bill.

FAIR DEBT COLLECTION PRACTICES ACT

If you begin getting collection calls from debt collectors tell them that the spouse (or parent as the case may be) is deceased. If they insist that it is a joint debt, do not pay anything on it until you have proof that you are legally responsible. Debt collectors will lie to you sometimes to try to get even partial payment. Sometimes they are working on a commission, getting a percentage of what they are able to collect. There is a federal statute, the Fair Debt Collection Practices Act, that regulates what they can and cannot do.

CHAPTER NINE

The Probate Court Process

Probate is the legal word for the process of proving the existence and validity of a last will and testament. If there is a will, the estate is called testate. If there is no will, the estate is deemed intestate. The difference between the two can determine who are the heirs and what are their individual shares of the estate, as well as any restrictions or conditions on receiving those shares. The probate process is much the same for both testate and intestate estates.

WILL VERSUS TRUST

A will is a written document that is governed by specific rules and procedures to make it comply with state law. It spells out who gets what and when and who is in charge of seeing that this happens. It can also be used to name a guardian for minor children. (Note: See the discussion of the living will, which is not a will at all.)

A trust is like a will in that it is a written document stating who gets what at the death of the trust maker and what restrictions, if any, are imposed on that distribution, and who is in charge of seeing that the trust instructions are carried out. But a trust does not have to go through the probate process and is not usually subject to the oversight of a probate court.

PROBATE PROCESS

It used to be that most all estates were settled by the probate process. Trusts were rarely used except for complicated and high-value estates with significant tax problems. This began to change in the mid-1960s when a non-attorney financial planner published a book promoting trusts as a substitute for wills. This got him in a lot of legal trouble with lawyers who complained of him engaging in the unauthorized practice of law. He was criminally prosecuted but had started a wave of followers who realized that trusts were an option and that a will was not the only way or even the best way to settle an estate.

Probate is in its simplest form a legal process overseen by a judge and a court. It consists of filing a series of fill-in-the-blank forms that enable the personal representative of an estate (who was either named in a will or appointed by a judge) to gather the assets of a deceased, pay any expenses to the court or lawyers or both, identify and pay claims of the estate, and finally to distribute the assets to either the named heirs in a will or to those who are legal heirs by law.

The reason lawyers are typically needed in a probate case nowadays is that they know which forms to file and the order in which they are filed according to the law and the court rules. The clerks of the probate court know all this too, but are not allowed to help anyone file the forms or explain anything about filling them out. Before there were preprinted, fill-in-the-blank forms, the lawyer's secretary would type the documents with the same information that now appears on the forms. Lawyers back then (pre-1960s) were needed because of their specialized knowledge of the law and the information needed on the filed documents.

But now we have the fill-in-the-blank forms. They are self-explanatory and well-liked by the court system since they have standardized the probate process, making it more efficient than before.

But the fact is that lawyers—many of them—still charge the same even though the process is far simpler than it was previously. In fact, attorney involvement is minimal in a simple probate case. The non-attorney legal assistant can enter the information needed on the computer and the printer will spit the filled-in forms out in a matter of minutes. They can then be signed by the personal representative, filed with the court, and copied to all interested parties with no attorney involvement at all. Yet when the billing arrives, the inference is that the lawyer did all of those things and should be paid for them at the normal hourly rate. Some states, Florida for instance, even prohibit anyone except lawyers to handle a simple probate case. There is no good reason why a surviving spouse or adult child cannot fill out the forms to do an entire probate case beginning to end with no lawyer involved at all. If they run into an issue then a lawyer can be called upon. Lots of states allow this. Enough said about that. Now I wait for the lawyer hate mail.

This is not to say there is no need for attorneys. Sometimes there are problems and conflicts. Claims against the estate may be disputed. The validity of a will might be questioned. The personal representative could be challenged if he or she does not seem to be doing the job in identifying, collecting, or distributing assets. The probate judges are not in danger of losing their jobs. It's just that in the majority of cases the attorneys and judges have little to do other than rubber-stamping the paperwork filed.

There are typically several ways to probate an estate using different procedural methods. Model laws such as the Uniform Probate Code has been adopted by eighteen states, and others have adopted parts of the UPC or the now popular Estates and Protected Individuals Code, EPIC. State courts typically offer more than one way to process a probate case. If the estate size is modest, a simple affidavit process might be suitable. In some states the attorney can choose to use the full supervised probate process, with the judge ruling in open court on major incidents in the process, such as approving the sale of real estate or the admission of the will. Or the attorney might use a simplified procedure that would allow the paperwork to flow and the estate assets to be distributed with no court involvement at all. Obviously, the simplified process should be less costly than the supervised probate process. But it is not always billed that way.

The basic steps in a probate are pretty much the same in most states, and the fact that the estate is testate or intestate doesn't change the process much. But there are sometimes significant differences in procedure and your attorney will know the correct process where the probate is being processed.

1. File the will, if any, with the court along with the form to commence probate proceedings and the form appointing the personal representative of the estate.
2. Notify all interested parties and publish notice to creditors.
3. Identify and value all the assets and transfer them to the estate name.
4. Open a bank account for the probate estate using the EIN from the IRS (see Chapter 10).
5. Prepare an inventory of all assets and their values. Note that in cases of personal property such as furniture and household goods, no one from the court comes to the house to conduct a separate inventory. They take your word for it.
6. Pay all taxes, inventory fees, court fees, attorneys' fees, and personal representative fees.
7. Transfer all liquid assets to the estate bank account.
8. Distribute the assets to the heirs. In-kind items can be given direct to heirs; others get cash/check/electronic bank transfer. They must sign a court form receipt for their share.
9. File notice of completion with court clerk. Sometimes a court hearing is necessary.

That's a simplified explanation and there are other forms that some states will require, but an Internet search will give you step-by-step procedures for the state of the deceased.

Small estate probate procedures are in effect in most states. This allows a one-step affidavit procedure to be used to transfer assets of smaller amounts to heirs without going through the multistep process above. I go into more detail about that in my book *How to Avoid Probate for Everyone*.

READING OF THE WILL

So many films, novels, and television shows depict the reading of the will that most people think the ceremony is a required part of the probate process. It isn't. While there are some lawyers who still gather the heirs together so everyone can find out who got what or who was disinherited, most of the time there is no formal will reading. However, heirs and interested parties as defined by law are required to be given a copy of the will within a stated time period, usually thirty days. In the case of a trust-based estate settlement, the portions of the trust relevant to a particular heir should be copied to them but not necessarily the entire trust document.

ADVANTAGES OF PROBATE

Probate is not always a bad word. Sometimes we need the authority of a judge to ensure that the probate proceedings are done honestly and efficiently. For example, there is a provision in the Model Trust Act that allows a judge to double damage awards against a person embezzling money from an estate, or against someone who refuses to turn over assets of the estate to a personal representative. (This is in addition to any applicable criminal charges.) A judge can resolve disputes among heirs for situations such as replacing a personal representative, ruling on the validity of a will, naming a guardian at law for minor or disabled heirs, and any other issue that needs to be adjudged.

It used to be that probate offered a short statute of limitations within which creditors had to file their claims or the claim was barred. That advantage was not available to trusts. Nowadays most states allow the same notice and claims period after publishing the trust claims notice as was once only available to probate. Attorneys would file a probate case even if not needed to distribute assets just so the trust would be under the same short time frame umbrella as a will. In most states that is no longer necessary.

SETTLING AN ESTATE WITH A REVOCABLE TRUST

What is a trust, you ask? A trust is in effect similar to a will. It addresses how trust assets will be distributed at the death of the trust owner and who is in charge of seeing that that happens. When you sign it, the trust becomes a legal entity—somewhat similar to a corporation with the ability to own things. Unlike a corporation there is no annual reporting requirements or separate taxes. The trust can own your house, your car, your business, even your furniture and household goods. But you own the trust, so nothing changes day-to-day. You can still sell your house, your car, or deal with the things you own in every way that you could without the trust. But at your death, the trust is still alive in a sense and still owns your stuff. At that point the person you appointed as trustee takes over and carries out your instructions, pays your bills, files your taxes, all without lawyers, courts, or the attendant waiting periods, delays, and expenses. Plus, it's all private, unlike probate, the records of which are open to the public. In probate anyone can look at the file and find out who inherited, how much they inherited, and their address. Not true with a trust, which is unregistered.

TESTAMENTARY TRUSTS VERSUS LIVING TRUSTS

An important distinction needs to be recognized between a testamentary trust and a living trust. A testamentary trust is one that is created after your death because your last will and testament directed that it be created after your death. For example, the will might say that the children of the deceased are to receive $50,000 each; but that if they are under a certain age, say for example twenty-five, then their share shall be held in trust for them to be used for living and educational expenses with any remaining funds given to them when they reach that age. The problem with the testamentary trust for children is that it has to go through probate to be created, requiring significant cost, and incurs additional costs for annual reporting and even court appearances until the given age.

There are attorneys who prefer the testamentary trust since they want the court supervision, and in some cases that might be a concern.

With a living trust there is no probate involvement, no costs, no waiting for probate to be completed, and the trustee has more discretion as to money management for the beneficiaries. For example, the living trust might say that the funds for the beneficiary can be used for educational, medical, and living expenses. The trustee is then the one who decides what expenses are reasonable and necessary. I had a case where the testamentary trust was for an eighteen-year-old who had just started college. She was requesting money for a car since it was less expensive to live off campus, but there was no public transportation. Her trustee, an uncle who had been appointed in the will, agreed to the need for a car, but the judge, who had to approve any such expense, refused the request, saying it was not technically for educational purposes. The fact was that the trust had several hundred thousand dollars in it and could well afford a car. Had the parent of the child used a living trust instead, no judge's approval would be needed and the trustee could have bought one for her.

What if there is a last will and testament but everything was either jointly owned or had named beneficiaries? In that case, even though there was a will and the deceased died testate, there is no need for probate in most cases, no matter what some attorneys might tell you. I have heard attorneys claim that probate is necessary even when there is a probate-avoiding trust in existence. They say that not everything is covered by the trust, such as household goods and personal property, since these have no written titles. However, with proper funding, there is typically a general assignment of assets to the trust from the grantor that serves as a catch-all for items with no title. With proper funding there is no need to probate the will.

A LIVING TRUST IS NOT A WILL

It is created by a different document, made and funded while the grantor (trust maker) is alive. At the death of the grantor, the trust provisions automatically kick in, and each share of each heir is managed by the trustee appointed in the trust document. There are no costs, no court supervision, no attorneys in most cases, and there is no long waiting period or delay as there can be with a testamentary trust. It is the preferred method for avoiding probate.

CHAPTER TEN

The Trust Settlement Process

Some of the steps below dealing with identifying, valuing, and transferring assets apply equally to probated estates as well as trust-based estates.

GET AN EMPLOYER IDENTIFICATION NUMBER

If the original trust owner (the grantor or trustor) hasn't already done it, go to the IRS website and get an EIN (www.irs-tax-ein-number.com; it's like a Social Security number is for a person). Use this to open bank accounts, sell real estate, or any activity where a Social Security number would otherwise be used. **You can no longer use the SS number of the deceased after their death.** After you have your EIN, you can use it to transfer assets into the trust.

BENEFICIARY ACCOUNTS

First, look at each account that might have either a beneficiary listed: a pay-on-death (POD) designation, a transfer on death (TOD) designation, or a co-owner. These assets could be in the form of a bank deposit account, brokerage account, bonds, life insurance, annuities, real estate, vehicles and boats, or assets that are being paid out in installments such as land contracts or even lottery winnings.

If there is a co-owner named, or a beneficiary who is anyone other than the trust, turn over the information on those assets to the co-owner or named beneficiary if that person is still alive.

If not, and there is an alternate beneficiary, the asset should be given to the alternate. They will make their own claim and it is not the job of the trustee to do that for them.

If the trust is named as the beneficiary or there is no named surviving beneficiary, then the trustee makes the claim for those assets on behalf of the trust. The procedure to get the asset to the trust depends upon the type of asset.

TRANSFER ON DEATH DEEDS; LADYBIRD DEED

Real estate can, in many states, have a TOD beneficiary. This type of deed says on its face that it is in the name of the owner, not the trust, but that if the owner dies before the beneficiary, the real estate belongs to the beneficiary. Prior to death the owner retains the right to revoke it, sell it, mortgage it, or list another beneficiary. The beneficiary has no rights at all to the property unless he or she survives the owner. In some states the deed must be filed and recorded with the court clerk or register of deeds prior to death to be legal. In other states the deed can be filed after death. This kind of deed is sometimes called a ladybird deed.

If there is a deed that transfers the property from the owner to the trust of the owner, with no beneficiary, the trustee can record the deed and then has full authority to follow the wishes of the grantor of the trust as to its disposition. In some states the deed must be filed prior to the death of the grantor, while in most states it can be filed at any time.

REAL ESTATE IN OTHER STATES; ANCILLARY PROBATE

If the grantor of the trust owned real estate in more than one state, it is very important to find the deeds to the trust for those properties and have them recorded in that state, preferably before the death of the grantor of the trust. Otherwise, the pour-over will (a will which leaves everything to the trust) of the grantor will have to go through what is called ancillary probate in the other states before the trustee can dispose of or transfer it. It is possible that with poor planning an estate could have to endure the cost and hassle of multiple probate proceedings. You should record a copy of the death certificate with the deeds office in the county of every state in which the deceased owned real estate. This helps avoid identity theft. I have seen cases where vacation homes of the deceased—often located in other states—were taken over by squatters and even rented out or sold.

If the deceased had no trust or if the property in the other state was not deeded to the trust, then the ancillary probate will likely be expensive since an attorney in that state will have to be paid to handle the probate and turn over the ownership to personal representative of the home state.

TIME-SHARES

Another asset that may actually turn out to be a liability is a time-share. Notify the time-share company of the death, but it is possible they may file a claim for amounts owed on the time-share contract. That contract should be reviewed by an attorney to determine the responsibility of the estate for that contract. A similar problem could exist for those with campground club memberships.

Another potential asset is country-club memberships. These often have been purchased with a substantial down payment and regular monthly payments. The contracts are sometimes able to be sold or transferred, so that paperwork should also be examined.

SEARCH FOR AND IDENTIFY
OTHER ASSETS AND DEBTS

Assets need to be valued in order to satisfy tax requirements, if any, and to be certain that the heirs receive the correct shares of the estate. This is especially true when in-kind distributions are to be made and the distribution instructions require a specific percentage of the estate to go to particular people. For real estate, an appraisal is appropriate. Other assets that are not to be liquidated need to be valued, even if the valuation is based upon an agreement of all heirs and interested parties. While it is not always required, good practice is to prepare a final inventory listing all assets and debts to keep the trust distribution transparent to the heirs.

LIQUIDATE ASSETS, PAY ALLOWABLE CLAIMS, DISTRIBUTE ASSETS TO HEIRS

Liquidate assets except for those to be given in kind to heirs. File taxes; pay allowable debts and expenses of administration. Then distribute assets to heirs according to terms of the trust document.

A trust might remain open to manage assets for heirs such as benefits for minors.

Once the trust has completed all the transfers and no longer owns any assets, it ceases to exist without filing any paperwork to that effect. Sometimes the trust will remain open in the event the share of an heir is to be held for that heir for a period of time. A minor child's share might be kept in trust to be used for educational expenses with the balance being distributed in full at a given age (attaining age twenty-five is a commonly used condition). The instructions for handling trust funds can be complicated or simple depending entirely on the wishes of the grantor. If the trust remains open and has taxable income, the trust itself must file a tax return using the EIN.

I go into quite a bit of detail about wrapping up the business of a trust in my book *Living Trusts for Everyone* (second edition). Of the 3,500-plus trusts I have created for clients over the years, I am happy to report no problems with the trust itself. Of course, there were a few rivalries and family arguments among heirs, but I suspect those would have been even worse had those estates gone through probate.

THE TRUST OR ESTATE BANK ACCOUNT

Whether the estate is handled by a trust or a probated will, the estate will need a bank account. You cannot use the existing bank account of the deceased for estate purposes. Joint bank accounts with the deceased and others are assumed to be owned by the co-owner until proven otherwise.

To open an estate bank account, you need the EIN and either your probate Letters of Authority or an Affidavit of Trust along with your personal identification and a death certificate. Some banks require a copy of the trust document itself. Do not give them the original; they may have a photocopy. This is to ensure them that you are in fact the personal representative or the successor trustee with the authority to deposit and withdraw funds from the account.

You can then use the account to deposit estate assets and pay estate expenses. Remember that you should not pay creditor claims until after the expiration of the time set in the Notice to Creditors, which should be filed as soon as possible after your appointment as the trustee or personal representative. If there are co-trustees or co-personal representatives, then both signatures would be required for any payments from the estate account.

PERSONAL PROPERTY—
WHO GETS THE STUFF AND HOW TO DECIDE

The biggest problem the administrator of an estate can have is usually what to do about all the personal belongings of a deceased. Unless there is a single heir (in which case that stuff is their problem), or unless the deceased provided specific instructions on who gets what, it is ultimately up to the personal representative or successor trustee to come up with a fair way to distribute or liquidate the personal property.

Sometimes the sheer volume of personal property is overwhelming. I have had to deal with estates of hoarders and heirs who couldn't agree on a plan or method, which resulted in no one being happy with the final solution. Here are some ideas that have worked in the past, and I find that if you present alternatives to the heirs with the implication that no agreement means that you alone decide, you can usually avoid a court fight.

ESTATE SALES, APPRAISALS, ONE-OF-A-KIND ITEMS

Special or one-of-a-kind items that more than one person wants can cause problems. There is only one wedding ring, and if there is more than one heir who thinks they should have it, you have a problem. Perhaps it was promised to someone. If everybody agrees, then that is that. But what about its monetary value? Typically, the deceased will specify that everything is to be divided equally. Does that mean everything has to be valued to achieve an equal dollar division? The fact is that the wedding ring is not going to be sold. It is an heirloom and may be passed on to others later on. I suggest that specific items that have family or sentimental value not be divided based on their dollar value. These can be set aside and divided differently than the mass of other personal property, furniture, and furnishings. Trying to value household goods is an imprecise act. That $3,000 couch they bought last month may only be worth a few hundred dollars now since it became a used couch as soon as it left the showroom floor.

Where there are multiple claimants for a single item, drawing lots is an option. It leaves the choice to chance, but using that method eliminates the problem of an aggressive heir pushing to get their own way. (I have seen heirs skip the funeral so they get first shot at taking items out of the house.) Drawing lots could be the short straw approach, numbered slips of paper drawn from a hat, or a flip of a coin, but no one can complain about unfairness.

Taking turns in selecting items is another way. Draw lots to determine the order of choice and then each person chooses one item, then the next person, and so on until there is nothing left that anyone covets. The balance can then be disposed of through auction, tag sale, a professional estate sales company, or a dumpster. The cost of a dumpster and fees for loading it are typically billed by the auction house or estate sale company.

As to estate sales companies, I have a caution. Some are not reputable and will separate obviously high-ticket items such as antiques for what they call private sale. You will have no control over what they sell it for or to whom. It may be to themselves at a bargain price. I have seen these companies require that the trustee or personal representative of the estate not attend the sale, claiming they don't want the family interfering with the sale process. This of course allows for more shenanigans if items are sold at less than fair market value to unknown buyers. If you go this way, be sure to attend the sale.

Most appraisers and auctioneers agree that collections be kept intact rather than treated as separate items. These might have considerable value (or none at all) so that should be considered and in some cases appraisals should be done.

Appraisals are easy to justify to heirs since taxes are sometimes assessed on the total value of the assets in the estate, and the personal representative or trustee is personally responsible to see that everything is valued properly. An objecting heir should be told: *It's not me, it's the law.*

Trustees and personal representatives (executors) are fiduciaries. This is a legal term that has the force of law. The fiduciary has to have an arm's-length relationship with the assets they are administering. They cannot personally profit either for themselves or friends and family from estate transactions. As I mentioned earlier, there are laws that allow for double damages and even criminal charges for breach of a fiduciary duty, such as embezzlement or self-dealing.

Ultimately, if there is no way to resolve a dispute among the heirs, the final say rests with the fiduciary, whose decision will likely stand up in court. The easiest decision, though sometimes harsh, and a real threat to recalcitrant heirs, is to sell everything and divide the money.

CHAPTER ELEVEN

Veterans' Benefits

If the deceased was a veteran, or the spouse or child of a veteran, there are benefits available to the heirs. Exactly what benefits can be claimed depends upon several factors. For most entitlements the veteran must have had an honorable discharge from the service.

BURIAL AND MEMORIAL BENEFITS

A burial plot is provided free in VA National Cemeteries for veterans and their spouses. In some cases, minor children are entitled also. Bad conduct can disqualify a veteran, including such things as the commission of a capital crime. See the appendix for detailed requirements. Note that not all costs of burial are necessarily covered.

BURIAL IN ARLINGTON NATIONAL CEMETERY

The rules are stricter for burial at Arlington National Cemetery. Aboveground burial (niche) is available for most honorably discharged veterans who served in active duty for at least one day. Casket burial in ground is at the discretion of the US Army, which oversees Arlington. In general, permission is given to those who died during active duty, or those who received the Medal of Honor, Distinguished Service Cross, Distinguished Service Medal, Silver Star or Purple Heart, or former prisoners of war. Call the cemetery for detail and current rules.

HEADSTONES, MARKERS, MEMORIAL FLAGS, MEDALLIONS

Headstones, markers, memorial flags, and medallions are also available on request. The request process is paperwork-heavy and I suggest talking first to the funeral home director since they are familiar with the procedures, costs, and benefits and can make the process much easier. You might also contact the local VA office as well as applying online at www.vets.gov.

In certain circumstances the VA will pay some of the funeral and burial expenses. The amount varies depending upon whether the death was while hospitalized in a VA hospital or if the deceased was receiving a VA pension or disability payments or if it was a service-related death and if interment was in a VA cemetery.

VETERAN'S PENSIONS AND LIFE INSURANCE

Veteran's pensions and life insurance are sometimes available to a surviving spouse and children, but there are lots of requirements that can disqualify you. The Office of Veterans Affairs, the Military Order of the Purple Heart, and your funeral home director can guide you through this.

If the veteran is a member of the Veterans of Foreign Wars, the local chapter should be contacted for the ritual service, firing squad salute, and casket bearers.

CHAPTER TWELVE

Social Security Survivors' Benefits

Social Security survivors' benefits can be very complex, depending upon the ages of the parties, their marital status, whether there are surviving minor children with or without a surviving spouse, whether the deceased was receiving Social Security disability benefits, and the earnings record of the deceased. The laws are in constant flux, and the very best advice is to make an appointment with the Social Security office and get current correct information as to your and your children's right to benefits. The information that follows is a general discussion of the current rules and laws for educational purposes and you should not rely on this information as a substitute for discussing your situation with the Social Security Administration. Further information and PDF booklets are available online at the government website: www.ssa.gov/benefits/survivors.

HOW TO APPLY

You cannot apply for any benefits including survivor's benefits via the Internet. Here is the information from Social Security as to application:

> *If you need to report a death or apply for benefits, call **1-800-772-1213** (TTY **1-800-325-0778**). You can speak to a Social Security representative between 8:00 a.m. – 7:00 p.m. Monday through Friday. You can find the phone number for your local office by using*

the Social Security Office Locator *and looking under Social Security Office Information. The toll-free "Office" number is your local office.*

IMMEDIATE CASH PAYMENT

A surviving spouse or, if none, surviving children can apply for a one-time payment of $255 as a cash benefit in addition to other survivor benefits. Your funeral director can assist you in making this application or you can call SSA to apply for it yourself.

WHO IS ENTITLED TO BENEFITS AS A SURVIVOR?

Surviving spouse, children, minor children, disabled spouses and disabled children, and ex-spouses of the deceased are entitled to benefits if they meet the SSA requirements.

HOW MUCH ARE SURVIVORS' BENEFITS?

The amount of the Social Security benefit is based on the amount the deceased person was receiving at the time of death. If benefits had not yet started, then the amount will be based on the amount of benefits to which the deceased would have been entitled based on prior earnings. The amount received by a surviving spouse depends upon several factors including the age of the spouse, whether there were any minor or disabled children, and whether the spouse is already receiving SS benefits. An eligible surviving ex-spouse married to the deceased for at least ten years would get the same amount as a current spouse. Whether to take the benefit depends upon whether it is more or less than the survivor would receive on their own account. Note that there is a family limit to the total amount paid to a surviving spouse and children, typically amounting to about 150 to 180 percent of the deceased's monthly benefit.

The Social Security office will help make that determination based on all available factors, including when you would expect to start receiving the benefits, so you do not need to pay anyone to examine your options.

An unmarried minor child can receive an amount equal to one-half that of the deceased parent who is receiving retirement or disability benefits, but if the other parent is also deceased the child can get 75 percent. The payments end at age eighteen, or at age nineteen if the child is attending high school. If the child is disabled, they do not end before the child reaches age twenty-two. If someone who does not qualify to get survivors' benefits is caring for a minor child who is entitled to benefits, the caretaker's benefit ceases when the child attains age sixteen.

Be sure to contact the Social Security office to get the current rules, qualification requirements, and benefit amounts rather than relying solely on the information here since rules change frequently.

HOW ARE BENEFITS PAID?

The benefits are paid monthly, by either check or direct deposit. This is the same method used for regular Social Security and disability benefits.

The benefits end at death, except for benefits paid to minors, which may end at age eighteen or nineteen; or upon a beneficiary marrying in some cases.

DISABILITY PAYMENTS, DIVORCE

If the deceased was receiving disability payments, are survivors entitled to anything?

Yes. If the surviving spouse is sixty years old or older or is disabled and is between ages fifty and sixty and has been married for at least one year, then the surviving spouse can get survivor's benefits. But if the survivor remarries before age sixty, or age fifty if disabled, Social Security benefits from the deceased spouse's account are stopped. Benefits can also be paid to a divorced ex-spouse at age sixty-two, provided they were married for at least ten years.

What if there is a divorced surviving spouse who was married to deceased ten years and there is also a current surviving spouse? Or what if there were several ten-year marriages with surviving former spouses? Is there a maximum?

An ex-spouse who was married for at least ten years who reaches full retirement age is entitled to 100 percent of the retirement benefit of the deceased spouse, and that amount is not reduced because there is another divorced surviving spouse or a current surviving spouse or both. They all get the full benefit. (Of course, even the most desirable mates can accumulate just so many ten-year marriages.)

CHAPTER THIRTEEN

Death Taxes

ESTATE TAXES

There is, in fact, a death tax. Commonly called an estate tax, it currently does not affect most estates. There are two kinds. The federal estate tax exemption amount has been raised to a level that only the very rich have to worry about it. For the year 2021, it does not affect estates worth less than $11.7 million. That's for those dying that year. There are ways to double that amount for a married couple and lots of tax strategies to minimize the tax owed, but that is for another book for those who have to worry about high-dollar estates.

The estate tax is paid by the estate to the IRS, whether there is probate or not. The tax rate can be pretty stiff, going from 18 percent to 40 percent of all amounts over the exemption limit. In general, surviving spouses do not pay an estate tax.

STATE INHERITANCE TAX

Six states have an **inheritance tax**, which is paid by the ones who inherit the assets. This money is paid to the individual state treasurer by the heirs. Sometimes the personal representative or trustee of the estate pays this and files the forms, then distributes the rest to the heirs. Here are the states with an inheritance tax and their current tax rates.

Iowa	5–15%
Kentucky	4–16%

Maryland	10%
Nebraska	1–18%
New Jersey	11–16%
Pennsylvania	4.5–15%

The reason most of these states have a range of fees is that the tax charged can vary depending upon your relationship to the deceased. Children may be charged a lower rate than siblings. There are exemptions from the inheritance tax that vary from state to state. Surviving spouses generally are exempt. Keep in mind that it is the state of the deceased's domicile that determines whether the tax is owed, not the state in which the beneficiary lives. If, for example, you live in California and your aunt from Iowa dies, you would owe the inheritance tax. But if the aunt lived in California and you in Iowa, no inheritance tax is due at all since California is a no-inheritance-tax state. Tax laws change often and the information here is not to be relied upon without checking current law first.

Life insurance is not taxed in any state and is not considered income by the IRS. If the life insurance proceeds are invested, then the interest earned by the life insurance proceeds is taxed.

ESTATE INCOME TAX

There are two income tax issues for the estate. If the estate assets are invested or income producing during the pendency of wrapping up the estate, then that income is taxed for federal, state, and local income tax (except where there is no state or local income tax). There is no standard deduction since the estate is not a person. Sometimes estates consist of ongoing businesses, stocks that produce dividends, interest income on estate accounts, and continuing royalty income.

If the estate stays open so long that the estate's assets earn income, then the estate has to file an estate tax return (using the EIN number referred to earlier). It doesn't matter whether the assets are in a trust or in probate. If income is earned, then taxes might be payable. An estate does not have a standard deduction as does an individual. The IRS 1041 form is for a domestic deceased's estate, trust, or bankruptcy estate. The form is required for estates earning $600 or more in taxable income. An estate must also pay quarterly estimated income tax payments in the same manner as individuals.

Like most of the tax code, a 1041 is complicated, and filing a 1041 with the required related schedules requires tax expertise best left to professionals.

DECEDENT'S LAST INCOME TAX

The second tax issue is the deceased's personal tax return for the year of death, including federal, state, and city taxes as applicable. If the deceased was married at time of death, the surviving spouse can elect to file as married filing jointly, which preserves the standard deduction or itemized deductions for the survivor. You as the surviving spouse would sign your name and write in the signature block for your spouse the following: "filing as the surviving spouse."

PROBATE COSTS AND FEES

When an estate is probated, the probate court in some states collects an inventory fee, which is sometimes a percentage of the value of the estate being probated. There are additional fees in most cases including filing fees, attorney fees, guardian ad litem fees, and fees of the personal representative. These are not called taxes, but since they are paid out of estate assets prior to distribution to the heirs, it amounts to the same thing.

The fees are paid through the probate process, but not all estate assets need to go through probate. For example, life insurance typically has a beneficiary and if so, is not part of the probated estate. The same is true of any pay-on-death or transfer-on-death account, including bank and investment accounts. However, if the insurance policy names the deceased's estate as the beneficiary, then it is part of probate. Jointly owned property such as real estate does not have to be probated in most cases.

An exception might be where the real estate is owned by multiple people as "tenants in common with no right of survivorship" and one of the joint owners dies. The share of that joint owner belongs to his estate and his heirs, not the other joint owners.

This differs from the type of ownership called "joint tenants with right of survivorship." In that case, at the death of one owner the other living owners now share the asset and the deceased owner's survivors get nothing.

The third type of ownership is where the property is owned jointly by a married couple, "tenancy by the entireties," where when one spouse dies the survivor gets full title to the property. Note that if the survivor remarries, the property is not automatically tenancy by the entireties with the new spouse. Unless a new deed is made from the surviving spouse to both partners saying specifically that it is entireties property, it remains separate property and may have to be probated. This is assumed if, for example, the new deed is made with the grantor being Mary Smith and the grantees being Mary Smith and John Smith, a married couple.

All this probate complication is another reason to use a trust and avoid probate, eliminating the probate costs. Trusts can have attorney fees and trustee fees, but it is not unusual to see the trust process completed by the heirs with none of those costs at all.

CHAPTER FOURTEEN

Wrapping Up the Estate; Distribution of Assets to Heirs

How and when to turn over the estate assets to the heirs depends very much on the written directions of the deceased and the makeup of the assets themselves. If it's all cash going to competent adult beneficiaries with no strings or conditions attached and all debts and taxes are paid, it's as simple as writing checks and getting receipts from the heirs for their shares. In probate there will likely be a closing statement to file to tell the court that the case is over. In a trust you just get the receipts and close the estate bank account.

I find that it is a comfort to heirs if the entire settlement process is transparent. This does not mean that the heirs have any decision-making role in the estate administration. The trustee or the personal representative is the fiduciary, accountable to the courts, laws, and heirs. If the trustee or personal representative refuses to communicate with the heirs, then suspicions of malfeasance or incompetence can suggest to heirs that "maybe we should have our own lawyer." Adding another lawyer or two to the process will result in additional costs, and likely additional delays to getting the estate settled.

ACCOUNTING TO HEIRS AND COURTS OF ASSETS, FEES, AND EXPENSES

In a probate case most courts require an accounting to be given to all heirs detailing all income, valuation of all assets, and an itemized listing of all debts and expenses paid by the estate. This would include the itemized attorney fee statement as well as that of the personal representative—not just a flat dollar amount for these. In some states the fees of a personal representative and attorney for the estate are set by statute. If that is the case, say that in the accounting so that heirs have full knowledge of how the fees were determined.

In trusts, most things are done independent of court supervision and not mandated by law, so complete disclosure is even more important. Heirs will be less likely to complain if you have kept them apprised of things as they progress. Sticker shock can cause an heir to run for help if the amount of fees is large and a complete surprise. Similarly, the valuation of assets which might have to be distributed in kind and which might be difficult or impossible to appraise should be a topic of discussion. If everyone is on the same page, then the wrapping-up process will go smoothly.

EARLY OR PARTIAL DISTRIBUTIONS TO HEIRS

Oftentimes there are considerable assets that have been brought into the estate, but the estate cannot be completely closed because of some outstanding issues. If, for example, there is a house that needs to be sold to complete things but a buyer has not yet been found, the estate cannot be closed. If none of the heirs want to take the house as part of their share, and they resist just transferring title into all the heirs' joint names, then you have to wait.

In the meantime, the house expenses have to be paid. Utilities, insurance, taxes, and upkeep would require a cash reserve from which to pay the expenses during the waiting period. But if the assets in the estate are substantial enough, then a reserve for expenses could be held in the estate account and the bulk of the estate could be transferred immediately to the heirs. In a probate situation, such a plan would likely have to be approved by the probate judge. They even have a form in some states called a Receipt for Distributive Share, which has a box to check for either a partial or complete receipt of share. In a trust situation the same form can be used as proof that the amount received was a partial or complete distribution to avoid misunderstandings.

UTMA OR UGMA ACCOUNTS

Minor children cannot be in charge of their own money. The person's legal guardian, usually a parent, is typically appointed to be their conservator—i.e., their money manager. The reason is that the person cannot legally enter into contracts until he or she reaches the age of majority, typically age eighteen to twenty-one. But minors are often named as heirs either by being specifically left assets in a will or trust, or because they were named as beneficiaries of life insurance or investment accounts, or, if there was no trust or will, because they are named as a class of heir named to inherit under state law.

State laws often offer an alternative to a court conservatorship appointment depending upon the amount being inherited. If the amount is modest, some states allow the money to be put into an account established under the state's Uniform Transfers to Minors Act (UTMA) or Uniform Gifts to Minors Act (UGMA) for the benefit of the child until they reach the age of majority. Another alternative if the amount to be inherited is $5,000 or less, depending upon the appropriate state statute, is to have their parent or legal guardian manage the money for them until they reach legal age, without having to open one of the special UTMA or UGMA accounts.

If the deceased had a revocable trust, the trust could direct how much a minor would inherit, who would be in charge of that money, and when and under what conditions the money could be used for the benefit of the minor or turned over outright. It is not unusual for a trust to direct the successor trustee to hold the inheritance beyond the age of majority but allow funds to be used for educational or medical expenses. The worst scenario is having a minor inherit with no restrictions and then blow all the money, leaving nothing to pay for college even if

they wanted to go. Using a formula like one-third of the principal distributed at age twenty-five, one-half the remainder at age
thirty, and the balance at age thirty-five ensures that if the first
couple of installments are wasted the heir will have time and
maturity to, we hope, not waste the final installment.

If a beneficiary of any age is deemed by a court to be mentally or physically incapacitated to the point that they cannot
make reasoned judgments or decisions about their assets, then
the person's court-ordered conservator can manage their inheritance for them under the guidance of the local probate court.
The deceased's trust, if any, could have provided for a successor
trustee to take care of that position and responsibility without
probate court involvement.

CHAPTER FIFTEEN

Attorneys

In the creation of estate plans and the settlement of estates, attorneys fall into two groups: those who specialize in estate planning and those who have clients who say they need a will, so the attorney obliges. Most states do not have so-called board-certified estate planning attorneys. In fact, all licensed attorneys can legally prepare wills and trusts and there is no real way to know their level of expertise. If money is no object, choosing a large law firm that has attorneys who do nothing but trusts and estates will probably get you a good result. But remember that the partners and associates work for the most part by the hour, and in many firms attorneys are being pushed to bill as many hours as possible.

FEES, HOURLY, FLAT RATE, PERCENTAGE

Probate and trust settlement can be billed by attorneys in a number of ways. Most use the hourly rate, which varies by the area of the country in which you live. Major metro areas have higher hourly rates than areas with lower costs of living. The rates can range from $300 to $500 for attorneys and $150 to $225 for non-attorney paralegal time. Perhaps it will be more or less where you live, but be sure to get the fee structure and agreement in writing and have periodic statements sent to you so you can see how it is going. Some people are surprised and upset to find that their attorney bills them for quick telephone calls. It is important then that you discuss with the attorney an estimate of the time involved in your estate settlement and whether there is any of it that you can do yourself if you are so inclined. There are now states in which an attorney can represent the estate in limited areas without having full blown start-to-finish attorney involvement.

A fixed flat rate is sometimes offered for simple estates. Experienced lawyers will be able to give you a close estimate as to cost once they know the basic facts of the deceased's situation. Was there a will or trust? A surviving spouse? An ongoing business? Real estate in more than one state? Minor or disabled heirs? Tax issues? These are all things that can impact the work that needs to be done. What if other things arise that were unexpected, requiring additional legal time? How will that be paid? Flat rates are generally more common in preparing an estate plan than for settling an estate.

The percentage fee is sometimes used, and in probate cases may be authorized by state law. Keep in mind though that an $800,000 estate may take the same attorney time for probate as a $150,000 one, so you may be overpaying on the higher asset case. Ask whether you have the option to go with hourly. Remember too that while most people don't ask, attorney fees are negotiable, especially in smaller firms.

Most parts of the country have an attorney or two who offer free seminars to set up a living trust and all the related documents. I have found that due to the volume of clients they serve they are also a reasonable choice to help settle an estate after the death of the trust grantor or will maker.

IS AN ATTORNEY NEEDED OR REQUIRED?

One thing you need to know is that in most states you do not need to have an attorney probate the estate. As I mentioned in an earlier chapter, unless there is litigation needed, an attorney is not needed to complete the probate process provided it is permissible under state law. Mostly it is a matter of using fill-in-the-blank forms. Remember, though, that the clerks at the courthouse are not going to tell you how to fill out the forms.

There are a few states where an attorney is required to probate the estate, the rationale being that a non-attorney filing probate paperwork is engaging in the unauthorized practice of law.

As for settling a trust estate, if you read my book, *Living Trusts for Everyone*, you will find a pretty easy-to-understand and simplified explanation of the settlement process. I have received many thanks from people who did this successfully themselves. At no cost to the estate.

CHAPTER SIXTEEN

What You Should Do to Make Your Own Estate Easy, Quick, and Inexpensive to Administer

Two things you should not do: Die without a trust and die thinking that a will is the way to settle your estate. Seriously, read my two books, *Living Trusts for Everyone* and *How to Avoid Probate for Everyone*.

You absolutely should try to avoid probate, and it does not have to be through using a living trust. You should also have the documents you need to cover permanent or temporary disability. A medical power of attorney, a business power of attorney, and a living will are documents that will assist your family in decision-making and doing for you what you cannot do for yourself.

Unmarried couples living together should be certain that each of you have named the other in the roles of agent for business and medical decision-making in the event you are unable to make those decisions for yourself. In your estate planning documents be sure that at the death of one of you the survivor is protected in rights to use or own living accommodations as well as access to your personal property.

One big problem is your personal stuff. Help out by getting organized to the extent possible. Clear out the clutter; make a list of what personal items should be given to which people or organizations. Make a list of passwords for your smartphone, tablet, and computer. Tell someone the combination to your safe. List your credit cards, bank and investment accounts, and all login names and passwords for your online accounts, email, and social media accounts. Keep all your insurance policies, deeds, and vehicle titles in one spot along with your birth certificate and passport. If you make a trust, keep it funded.

You won't be there to hear them, but your heirs will thank you for it.

FORM LETTERS
AND SAMPLE FORMS

The following form letters and sample forms are provided for educational purposes and are not intended to act as legal advice. While these work for most areas, I cannot guarantee what particular rules and laws may require different things where you live. Often organizations will respond to a form letter by sending you their own forms to fill out, so these may act to help initiate the process rather than completing it. Before relying on these, be sure to get the advice of an attorney in your area.

The addresses, when present, were current at press time, but should be checked. These letters may be too small to photocopy, but retyping is easy enough.

A. Notice to Creditors: Decedent's Trust Estate or Decedent's Probate Estate. (This is published once in the local newspaper where the deceased lived. In some states, publishing this notice creates a short statute of limitations for potential or unknown creditors. Ask your attorney about the legal efficacy of this form in the jurisdiction of the deceased. Also check the deadline date in your state for presentment of claims, since it may not be four months as is shown on the examples.)

B. Funeral and Burial Arrangements. (You, as the grantor, should fill out this form for the use of your trustee so that your wishes are known and any prepaid items are revealed to the family.)

C. Obituary. (This is a matter of personal preference and local custom. Often funeral homes will have formats, but this gives you a place to start.)

D. Letter to Life Insurance Company.

E. Letter to Social Security.

F. Letter to Health Insurance Company.

G. Letter to Department of Veterans Affairs.

H. Letter to Organizations. (Often membership organizations have group benefit programs that may offer death benefits or services to the family.)

I. Letter to Civil Service Commission.

J. Letter to Employer.

K. Receipt for Distributive Share. (To be signed by any beneficiary and retained by the trustee as a receipt when the trustee distributes assets.)

L. Information for Death Certificate.

M. Notice of Appointment and Duties of Personal Representative.

N. Do Not Resuscitate Order.

A. NOTICE TO CREDITORS: DECEDENT'S TRUST ESTATE

TRUST ESTATE OF _____
(name of deceased)

To all creditors:
NOTICE TO CREDITORS: The decedent, _____
(name of deceased)
who lived at _____
(address of deceased),
died on _____ 20_____ .

Creditors of the decedent are notified that all claims against the trust estate will be forever barred unless presented to
_____, the successor trustee named in
The Revocable
(name of deceased)

Living Trust established by decedent on the
_____ day of _____ , 20_____ .
All such claims must be presented to the said successor trustee within 4 months after the date of publication of this notice.

_____   _____

Date   Trustee Name

        _____

        Address

        _____

        Telephone

PUBLISH ABOVE INFORMATION ONLY
Publish one time in _____
Name of Newspaper
Furnish Affidavit of Publication and statement of publication charges to the trustee whose address is above.

A.2 NOTICE TO CREDITORS: DECEDENT'S PROBATE ESTATE

PROBATE ESTATE OF _____
                        (name of deceased)

To all creditors:

NOTICE TO CREDITORS: The decedent, _____
                          (name of deceased)
who lived at _____
(address of deceased),
died on _____ 20_____ .

Creditors of the decedent are notified that all claims
against the probate estate will be forever barred unless
presented to _____, the Personal
Representative appointed by the _____ Court,
file # _____ on the _____ day of
_____ , 20_____ .
All such claims must be presented to the said Personal
Representative within 4 months after the date of publication
of this notice.

_____   _____

Date   Personal Representative Name

                               _____

                               Address

                               _____

                               Telephone

PUBLISH ABOVE INFORMATION ONLY
Publish one time in _____
                    Name of Newspaper
Furnish Affidavit of Publication and statement of publication
charges to the Personal Representative whose address is above.

B. FUNERAL AND BURIAL ARRANGEMENTS

Prepaid items and location; also include location of supporting paperwork:

Item location _____

Cemetery lot _____

Headstone _____

Location of funeral contract or name of funeral home

_____

Persons or organizations to notify (including Department of Veterans Affairs and organizations such as Masons who you may want to be involved in the funeral ceremony. You may want to attach a list of other people with contact information if these are not known by your family.):

_____

_____

_____

_____

Church or religious organization to which you belong:

_____

Who would you like to officiate at a funeral ceremony?

_____

Specific burial instructions (such as whether or not you want cremation or where you would like to be buried, or type of ceremony, open or closed casket, graveside ceremony, military or organization ceremony such as the Masonic Order):

_____

Cemetery plot location (or desired location to purchase a plot):

_____

Deed to the plot location if any is located here:

_____

Church/synagogue to notify:

_____

Date _____ Your Signature _____

C. OBITUARY

An obituary has several standard formats, varying by region of the country, religious orientation, and family tradition. Most newspapers will print whatever you decide to write. Some papers run these for free, while others charge you based on how long the obituary is and how many days it is to run. Online registries are also available.

Here is the traditional simplified format, though this can run longer or even shorter.

John William Jones, age 89, died Saturday, March 12, in Ann Arbor, Michigan.

Services will be held at the Moore Funeral Home on March 16 at 2:00 p.m., followed by burial at Sunset Gardens Park, where a graveside service will be held.

John was a member of Westside Church and retired from Ford Motor Company. He is survived by his wife Barbara and his two children, Nathan and Kristine.

Memorial contributions may be made to the National Heart Fund.

D. LETTER TO LIFE INSURANCE COMPANY

Date: _____

Name and Address of Insurance Company

Dear Sir or Madam:

Re: _____

(Insert Name of Deceased)

Date of Death _____

The above-named person had a policy with your company.

Policy Number _____

Please send me information on the death benefits or accrued benefits during the lifetime of the deceased and all claim forms needed to claim these benefits.

Please let me know what other information or documents you may need me to provide.

_____

Your Signature

_____

Print Name

Your Address

Your Telephone and Email

E. LETTER TO SOCIAL SECURITY

Date: _____

Social Security Administration

Address of Local Social Security Office

Dear Sir or Madam:

Re: _____

(Insert Name of Deceased)

Date of Death _____

Social Security Number _____

I am writing to inform you of the death of the above person. A copy of the death certificate is enclosed. I would like to arrange a meeting to discuss the options and benefits available to the surviving spouse and/or family.

Please either call me or let me know how to proceed to set up such a meeting.

Thank you for your help.

_____

Your Signature

_____

Print Name

Your Address

Your Telephone and Email

F. LETTER TO HEALTH INSURANCE COMPANY

Date: _____

Name and Address of Insurance Company

Dear Sir or Madam:

Re: _____

(Insert Name of Deceased)

Date of Death _____

The above-named person had a policy with your company.

Policy Number _____

Please send me information on the death benefits or accrued benefits during the lifetime of the deceased and all claim forms needed to claim these benefits.

Please let me know what other information or documents you may need me to provide.

_____

Your Signature

_____

Print Name

Your Address

Your Telephone and Email

G. LETTER TO DEPARTMENT OF VETERANS AFFAIRS

Date: _____

Department of Veterans Affairs
Insurance Division
500 Wissahickon Avenue or Fort Snelling
Philadelphia, PA 19010 St. Paul, MN 55111
Re: _____
(Insert Name of Deceased)
Date of Death _____

Dear Sir or Madam
I represent the estate of the above-named person whose Social Security Number is _____.

I have enclosed a photocopy of the death certificate.

He may have had insurance or other benefits due to him; please let me know what was available and the forms or procedures to claim those benefits.

The information I have is as follows:
Branch of Service _____.
Date of Entering Service _____
Discharge Date _____
Service Number (if different than Social Security Number)
_____

Please let me know what other information or documents you may need me to provide.

_____
Your Signature

_____
Print Name
Your Address
Your Telephone and Email

H. LETTER TO ORGANIZATIONS

Date: _____

Name and Address of Organization
Re: _____
(Insert Name of Deceased)
Date of Death _____

Dear Sir or Madam:
I represent the estate of the above-named person whose Social Security Number is _____.

I have enclosed a photocopy of the death certificate.

Please let me know what benefits may be available to the deceased and/or his or her family, including such things as life insurance, disability, vacation and sick pay, retirement, or other benefits. If there are claim forms for these please send them to me or let me know how to get them.

Please let me know what other information or documents you may need.

Sincerely,

_____

Your Signature

_____

Print Name
Your Address
Your Telephone and Email

I. LETTER TO CIVIL SERVICE COMMISSION

Date: _____

Civil Service Commission

1900 East Street, NW

Washington, D.C. 20415

Re: _____

(Insert Name of Deceased)

Date of Death _____

Dear Sir or Madam:

I represent the estate of the above-named person whose Social Security Number is _____.

I have enclosed a photocopy of the death certificate.

Please let me know what benefits may be available to the deceased and/or his or her family, including such things as life insurance, disability, vacation and sick pay, retirement, or other benefits. If there are claim forms for these please send them to me or let me know how to get them.

Please let me know what other information or documents you may need.

Sincerely,

_____

Your Signature

_____

Print Name

Your Address

Your Telephone and Email

J.   LETTER TO EMPLOYER

Date: _____

Name of Employer _____

Address _____

_____

Dear Sir or Madam:

I represent the estate of your employee/former employee

whose name is _____

and whose Social Security Number is _____

Please let me know if there are any accrued and unpaid
benefits available or payable to his or her estate. This might
include unpaid vacation or sick pay, group life insurance,
pension or retirement benefits, stock options or stock purchase
plans, profit sharing, disability income, payroll savings, or any
other benefits. If the deceased left personal property in your
possession, please let me know how to arrange for pickup.

Also, if there are claim forms available to access these
benefits, could you please forward those or tell me how to get
them.

I have enclosed a photocopy of the death certificate.

Please let me know what other information or documents
you may need.

Sincerely,

_____

Trustee/Personal Representative Signature

_____

Print Name
Address
Telephone and Email

K. RECEIPT FOR DISTRIBUTIVE SHARE OF TRUST OR PROBATE ESTATE

I hereby acknowledge the receipt of the following asset(s) from the following trust estate: _____
_____.

Name and Date of Trust
Description of asset(s) received:

This is a _____ full or _____ partial distribution to me from the estate.

I acknowledge that I have received a copy of the trust document as well as an accounting of trust assets and expenditures to date and am satisfied with the same.

Dated: _____

_____
Signature

_____
Print Name

L. INFORMATION FOR DEATH CERTIFICATE

Full Legal Name
Date of Birth
Sex
Date of Death
Name at Birth
Age Last Birthday
Location of Death
City, Village, Township of Death
County of Death
Current Residence Address
Social Security Number
Educational Level Achieved
Race
Ancestry
Ever in Armed Forces ?
Usual Occupation
Kind of Business/Industry
Marital Status
Name of Surviving Spouse
Father's Name
Mother's Name Before First Marriage

The balance of the death certificate will be completed by the
attending physician or medical examiner. This list may be
more or less information needed in the state where the person
died.

M.

(This is a required form used in most probate courts to notify heirs of the pendency of unsupervised probate. The forms will differ among states. If this is a trust settlement rather than a probate case, a letter will suffice in most states. The attorney, if there is one, typically fills out this form and sends it to heirs. In most states these forms are available from the court clerk's office.)

Notice of Appointment and Duties of Personal Representative

TO ALL INTERESTED PERSONS:

1. On _____ 20____ I was appointed personal representative as requested in the application or petition for probate of this estate:

    (copy attached unless previously sent).

I am serving without bond/with bond in the amount of $ _____.

    The papers related to the estate are on file with the County Probate Court located at _____

_____.

2. This is /is not a supervised administration.

    Attached is a copy of the will of the decedent which was /was not admitted to probate and under which I will administer, manage, and distribute the estate.

3. The court does not supervise the personal representative in the administration of an estate except in limited circumstances.

4. If I was appointed informally, you or another interested person may petition the court objecting to my appointment and/or demanding that I post a bond or an additional bond.

The petition must be filed with the probate court along with the applicable fee. Unless the court grants the petition, I will continue to serve as appointed.

5. You or another interested person may petition for a hearing by the court on any matter at any time during the administration of the estate, including for distribution of assets and allowance of expenses of administration. The petition must be filed with the probate court along with the applicable fee.

6. If you continue to be an interested person (such as an heir of an intestate estate or devisee or beneficiary under the will of the decedent), I will provide you with:
   a) a copy of the inventory within 91 days of my appointment;
   b) unless waived by you, a copy of an account including fiduciary fees and attorney fees charged to the estate, within 1 year of my appointment; and
   c) a copy of the closing statement or settlement petition when the estate is ready for closing.

7. To avoid penalties, I must have paid any federal estate and state estate taxes within 9 months after the date of the decedent's death or another time period specified by law.
8. The estate may not be closed earlier than 5 months after the date of my appointment except in limited circumstances. If the estate is not settled within 1 year after my appointment, within 28 days after the anniversary of the appointment, I must file with the court and send to each interested person a notice that the estate remains under administration and the reason for the continuation of the estate. If you do not receive such a notice, you may petition the court for a hearing on the necessity for continued administration or for closure of the estate.

_____   _____
Attorney   Personal Representative

_____

_____

Address   Address

_____

_____

Telephone   Telephone

ATTENTION: The above duties are not the only duties
required of the personal representative. This notice of
appointment must be served on all interested persons within
14 days after the appointment of the personal representative.
PC 573 (9/06) NOTICE OF APPOINTMENT AND
DUTIES OF PERSONAL REPRESENTATIVE Estate of
Approved, SCAO JIS CODE: NIP S

N. DO NOT RESUSCITATE ORDER

I request that in the event my heart and breathing should stop, no person shall attempt to resuscitate me.

This order is effective until it is revoked by me.

Being of sound mind, I voluntarily execute this order, and I understand its full import.

Signature _____

Type or print name _____

Date signed _____

ATTESTATION OF WITNESSES

The individual who has executed this order on this date and in our presence appears to be of sound mind and under no duress, fraud, or undue influence.

Signature _____

Type or print witness name _____

Date signed _____

Signature _____

Type or print witness name _____

Date signed _____

APPENDICES

1. Appendix A. Michigan Statute on Priority of Claims in Probate
   a. Homestead allowance
   b. Family allowance
   c. Exempt property
2. Appendix B. Probate. Priority of claim payments; insufficient assets
3. Appendix C. Federal Trade Commission Fair Debt Collection Practices Act
4. Appendix D. The Federal Trade Commission Funeral Rule
5. Appendix E. Durable Power of Attorney
6. Appendix F. Durable Power of Attorney for Health Care
7. Appendix G. Living Will and Declaration to Physicians
8. Appendix H. Certification from the Heir to a Vehicle
9. Appendix I. IRA and Deferred Compensation Rollovers
10. Appendix J. Required Minimum Distributions
11. Appendix K. Social Security Survivors Benefits
12. Appendix L. Department of Veterans Affairs Benefits
13. Appendix M. Deactivating or Memorializing Digital Presence
14. Appendix N. Assets Checklist

APPENDIX A

Michigan Statute on Priority of Claims in Probate

Section 700.3805 PART 4 Exempt Property and Allowances
Sec. 2401. This part applies to the estate of a deceased who dies domiciled in this state. For a deceased who dies domiciled outside of this state, rights to homestead allowance, family allowance, and exempt property are governed by the law of the deceased's domicile at death. History: 1998, Act 386, Eff. Apr. 1, 2000. Popular name: EPIC

a. 700.2402 Homestead allowance.
Sec. 2402. A deceased's surviving spouse is entitled to a homestead allowance of $24,000.00, adjusted as provided in section 1210. If there is no surviving spouse, each minor child and each dependent child of the deceased is entitled to a homestead allowance equal to $24,000.00, adjusted as provided in section 1210, divided by the number of the deceased's minor and dependent children. The homestead allowance is exempt from and has priority over all claims against the estate, except administration costs and expenses and reasonable funeral and burial expenses. A homestead allowance is in addition to any share passing to the surviving spouse or minor or dependent child by the will of the deceased, unless otherwise provided, by intestate succession, or by elective share. History: 1998, Act 386, Eff. Apr. 1, 2000; Am. 2000, Act 177, Imd. Eff. June 20, 2000. Popular name: EPIC

b. 700.2403 Family allowance.

Sec. 2403. (1) For their maintenance during the period of administration, a reasonable family allowance is payable to the deceased's surviving spouse and minor children whom the deceased was obligated to support, and children of the deceased or another who were in fact being supported by the deceased, which allowance shall not continue for longer than 1 year if the estate is inadequate to discharge allowed claims. The family allowance may be paid in a lump sum or in periodic installments. The family allowance is payable to the surviving spouse, if living, for the use of the surviving spouse and minor and dependent children; otherwise to the children or persons having their care and custody. If a minor child or dependent child is not living with the surviving spouse, the allowance may be paid partially to the child or to a fiduciary or other person having the child's care and custody, and partially to the spouse, as their needs may appear. (2) The family allowance is exempt from and has priority over all claims except administration costs and expenses, reasonable funeral and burial expenses, and the homestead allowance. The family allowance is not chargeable against a benefit or share passing to the surviving spouse or children by the will of the deceased, unless otherwise provided, by intestate succession, or by way of elective share. The death of an individual entitled to family allowance terminates the right to allowances not yet paid. History: 1998, Act 386, Eff. Apr. 1, 2000; Am. 2000, Act 177, Imd. Eff. June 20, 2000. Popular name: EPIC 700.2404

c. Exempt property. Sec. 2404.

(1) The deceased's surviving spouse is also entitled to household furniture, automobiles, furnishings, appliances, and personal effects from the estate up to a value not to exceed $16,000.00 more than the amount of any security interests to which the property is subject. If there is no surviving spouse, the deceased's children who are not excluded under subsection

(4) are entitled jointly to the same value. (2) If encumbered assets are selected and the value in excess of security interests, plus that of other exempt property, is less than $16,000.00, or if there is not $16,000.00 worth of exempt property in the estate, the spouse or children who are not excluded under subsection (4) are entitled to other assets of the estate, if any, to the extent necessary to make up the $16,000.00 value.

(2) Rights to exempt property and assets needed to make up a deficiency of exempt property have priority over all claims against the estate, except that the right to assets to make up a deficiency of exempt property abates as necessary to permit payment of all of the following in the following order: (a) Administration costs and expenses. (b) Reasonable funeral and burial expenses. (c) Homestead allowance. (d) Family allowance.

(3) The rights under this section are in addition to a benefit or share passing to the surviving spouse or children by the deceased's will, unless otherwise provided, by intestate succession, or by elective share.

The $16,000.00 amount described in this section must be adjusted as provided in section 1210. (4) The deceased may exclude 1 or more of the deceased's children from receiving exempt property or assets to make up a deficiency of exempt property under subsection (1) by either of the following means: (a) The deceased by will expressly states either of the following: (i) The child takes nothing. (ii) The child takes an amount of $10.00 or less from the estate. (b) The deceased by will expressly states that the child is not to receive exempt property under this section. History: 1998, Act 386, Eff. Apr. 1, 2000; Am. 2000, Act 177, Imd. Eff. June 20, 2000; Am. 2018, Act 143, Eff. Aug. 8, 2018. Popular name: EPIC

700.2405 Selection, determination, and documentation.
Sec. 2405. (1) If the estate is otherwise sufficient, property specifically devised shall not be used to satisfy rights to homestead allowance or exempt property. Subject to this restriction, the surviving spouse, fiduciaries, or others that have the care and custody of minor children, or children who are adults,

may select property of the estate as homestead allowance and exempt property. (2) The personal representative may make those selections if the surviving spouse, the adult children, or those acting for the minor children are unable or fail to do so within a reasonable time. The personal representative may execute a deed of distribution or other instrument to establish the ownership of property taken as homestead allowance or exempt property. The personal representative may determine the family allowance in a lump sum not exceeding $29,000.00, adjusted as provided in section 1210, or periodic installments not exceeding 1/12 of that amount per month for 1 year, and may disburse funds of the estate in payment of the family allowance and any part of the homestead allowance payable in cash. (3) The personal representative or an interested person aggrieved by a selection, determination, payment, proposed payment, or failure to act under this section may petition the court for appropriate relief, which may include a family allowance other than that which the personal representative determined or could have determined.

Probate. Priority of Claim Payments; Insufficient Assets

ESTATES AND PROTECTED INDIVIDUALS CODE
(EXCERPT)
Act 386 of 1998

700.3805 Priority of claim payments; insufficient assets.
(1) If the applicable estate property is insufficient to pay all claims and allowances in full, the personal representative shall make payment in the following order of priority:

(a) Costs and expenses of administration.

(b) Reasonable funeral and burial expenses.

(c) Homestead allowance.

(d) Family allowance.

(e) Exempt property.

(f) Debts and taxes with priority under federal law, including, but not limited to, medical assistance payments that are subject to adjustment or recovery from an estate under section 1917 of the social security act, 42 USC 1396p.

(g) Reasonable and necessary medical and hospital expenses of the deceased's last illness, including a compensation of persons attending the deceased.

(h) Debts and taxes with priority under other laws of this state.

(i) All other claims.

(2) A preference shall not be given in the payment of a claim over another claim of the same class, and a claim due and payable is not entitled to a preference over a claim not due.

(3) If there are insufficient assets to pay all claims in full or to satisfy homestead allowance, family allowance, and exempt property, the personal representative shall certify the amount and nature of the deficiency to the trustee of a trust described in section 7605(1) for payment by the trustee in accordance with section 7606. If the personal representative is aware of other non-probate transfers that may be liable for claims and allowances, then, unless the will provides otherwise, the personal representative shall proceed to collect the deficiency in a manner reasonable under the circumstances so that each non-probate transfer, including those made under a trust described in section 7605(1), bears a proportionate share or equitable share of the total burden.

The deceased may exclude 1 or more of the deceased's children from receiving exempt property or assets to make up a deficiency of exempt property under subsection (1) by either of the following means: (a) The deceased by will expressly states either of the following: (i) The child takes nothing. (ii) The child takes an amount of $10.00 or less from the estate. (b) The deceased by will expressly states that the child is not to receive exempt property under this section. History: 1998, Act 386, Eff. Apr. 1, 2000; Am. 2000, Act 177, Imd. Eff. June 20, 2000; Am. 2018, Act 143, Eff. Aug. 8, 2018. Popular name: EPIC 700.2405 Selection, determination, and documentation. Sec. 2405. (1) If the estate is otherwise sufficient, property specifically devised shall not be used to satisfy rights to homestead allowance or exempt property. Subject to this restriction, the surviving spouse, fiduciaries, or others that have the care and custody of minor children, or children who are adults may select property of the estate as homestead allowance and exempt property. (2) The personal representative may make those selections if the surviving spouse, the adult children, or those acting for the minor children are unable or fail to do so within a reasonable time. The personal representative may execute a deed of distribution or other instrument to establish the ownership of property taken as homestead allowance or exempt property. The personal representative may determine the family allowance in a lump sum not exceeding $18,000.00, adjusted as provided in section 1210, or periodic installments not exceeding 1/12 of that amount per month for 1 year, and may disburse funds of the estate in payment of the family allowance and any part of the homestead allowance payable in cash. (3) The personal representative or an interested person aggrieved by a selection, determination, payment, proposed payment, or failure to act under this section may petition the court for appropriate relief, which may include a family allowance other than that which the personal representative determined or could have determined. History: 1998, Act 386, Eff. Apr. 1, 2000. Popular name: EPIC

Federal Trade Commission Fair Debt Collection Practices Act

At the death of a loved one, the last thing grieving family members want are calls from debt collectors asking them to pay a loved one's debts. As a rule, those debts are paid from the deceased person's estate.

According to the Federal Trade Commission (FTC), the nation's consumer protection agency, family members typically are not obligated to pay the debts of a deceased relative from their own assets. What's more, family members—and all consumers—are protected by the federal Fair Debt Collection Practices Act (FDCPA), which prohibits debt collectors from using abusive, unfair, or deceptive practices to try to collect a debt.

Under the FDCPA, a debt collector is someone who regularly collects debts owed to others. This includes collection agencies, lawyers who collect debts on a regular basis, and companies that buy delinquent debts and then try to collect them.

Does a debt go away when the debtor dies?
No. The estate of the deceased person owes the debt. If there isn't enough money in the estate to cover the debt, it typically goes unpaid. But there are exceptions to this rule. You may be responsible for the debt of the deceased person if you:

- cosigned the obligation;
- live in a community property state, such as California;

- are the deceased person's spouse and state law requires you to pay a particular type of debt, like some health care expenses; or
- were legally responsible for resolving the estate and didn't comply with certain state probate laws.

If you have questions about whether you are legally obligated to pay a deceased person's debts from your own assets, talk to a lawyer.

Who has the authority to pay the deceased person's debt out of his or her assets?

The person named in a will who is responsible for settling a deceased person's affairs is called the executor. If there is no will, the court may appoint an administrator, personal representative, or universal successor, and give them the authority to settle the affairs. In some states, others (or other people) may have that authority, even if they haven't been formally appointed by the court.

Whom may a debt collector talk to about a deceased person's debt?

Under the FDCPA, collectors can contact and discuss the deceased person's debts with that person's spouse, parent(s) (if the deceased was a minor child), guardian, executor, or administrator. Also, the FTC permits collectors to contact any other person authorized to pay debts with assets from the deceased person's estate. Debt collectors may not discuss the debts of deceased persons with anyone else.

If a debt collector contacts a deceased person's relative, what can they talk about?

Collectors are allowed to contact third parties (such as a relative) to get the name, address, and telephone number of the deceased person's spouse, executor, administrator, or other person authorized to pay the deceased's debts. Collectors usually are permitted to contact such third parties only once to get this information. The main exception is if a collector reasonably believes that the information provided initially was inaccurate or incomplete, and that the third party now has more accurate or complete information. However, collectors cannot say anything about the debt to the third party.

Even if I am authorized to pay a deceased person's debt, can I stop a debt collector from contacting me about the debt?
Yes. To exercise this right, you must send a letter to the collector stating that you do not want the collector to contact you again. A telephone call is not enough. Make a copy of your letter for your files, send the original by certified mail, and pay for a "return receipt" so you can document what the collector received and when. Once the collector gets your letter, he cannot contact you again except to confirm that there will be no further contact or that he or the creditor plans to take a specific action, like filing a lawsuit to collect the debt. Keep in mind that even if you stop collectors from communicating with you, you are still responsible for the debt.

Report any problems you have with a debt collector to your state attorney general's office at naag.org and the Federal Trade Commission at ftccomplaintassistant.gov. Many states have their own debt collection laws that are different from the federal FDCPA. Your attorney general's office can help you determine your rights under your state's law.

Federal Trade Commission Funeral Rule

The Funeral Rule, enforced by the Federal Trade Commission (FTC), makes it possible for you to choose only those goods and services you want or need and to pay only for those you select, whether you are making arrangements when a death occurs or in advance. The rule allows you to compare prices among funeral homes, and makes it possible for you to select the funeral arrangements you want at the home you use. (The rule does not apply to third-party sellers, such as casket and monument dealers, or to cemeteries that lack an on-site funeral home.)

Your Rights Under the Funeral Rule
The Funeral Rule gives you the right to:
- **Buy only the funeral arrangements you want.** You have the right to buy separate goods (such as caskets) and services (such as embalming or a memorial service). You do not have to accept a package that may include items you do not want.
- **Get price information on the telephone.** Funeral directors must give you price information on the telephone if you ask for it. You don't have to give them your name, address, or telephone number first. Although they are not required to do so, many funeral homes mail their price lists, and some post them online.

- **Get a written, itemized price list when you visit a funeral home.** The funeral home must give you a General Price List (GPL) that is yours to keep. It lists all the items and services the home offers, and the cost of each one.
- **See a written casket price list before you see the actual caskets.** Sometimes, detailed casket price information is included on the funeral home's GPL. More often, though, it's provided on a separate casket price list. Get the price information before you see the caskets, so that you can ask about lower-priced products that may not be on display.
- **See a written outer burial container price list.** Outer burial containers are not required by state law anywhere in the United States, but many cemeteries require them to prevent the grave from caving in. If the funeral home sells containers, but doesn't list their prices on the GPL, you have the right to look at a separate container price list before you see the containers. If you don't see the lower-priced containers listed, ask about them.
- **Receive a written statement after you decide what you want, and before you pay.** It should show exactly what you are buying and the cost of each item. The funeral home must give you a statement listing every good and service you have selected, the price of each, and the total cost immediately after you make the arrangements.
- **Get an explanation in the written statement from the funeral home that describes any legal cemetery or crematory requirement** that requires you to buy any funeral goods or services.
- **Use an "alternative container" instead of a casket for cremation.** No state or local law requires the use of a casket for cremation. A funeral home that offers cremations must tell you that alternative containers are available, and must make them available. They might be made of unfinished wood, pressed wood, fiberboard, or cardboard.
- **Provide the funeral home with a casket or urn you buy elsewhere.** The funeral provider cannot refuse to handle a

casket or urn you bought online, at a local casket store, or somewhere else—or charge you a fee to do it. The funeral home cannot require you to be there when the casket or urn is delivered to them.

- **Make funeral arrangements without embalming.** No state law requires routine embalming for every death. Some states require embalming or refrigeration if the body is not buried or cremated within a certain time; some states don't require it at all. In most cases, refrigeration is an acceptable alternative. In addition, you may choose services like direct cremation and immediate burial, which don't require any form of preservation. Many funeral homes have a policy requiring embalming if the body is to be publicly viewed, but this is not required by law in most states. Ask if the funeral home offers private family viewing without embalming. If some form of preservation is a practical necessity, ask the funeral home if refrigeration is available.

Durable Power of Attorney

KNOW ALL MEN BY THESE PRESENTS, that I, _____, SS# _____, residing at this address: _____ _____, hereby revoke any general power of attorney that I have heretofore given to any person, and by these Presents do constitute, make and appoint, my true and lawful attorney. If _____ is unable or unwilling to act for me, then I appoint _____ as my true and lawful attorney.

(Include the following paragraph if the POA is springing—that is, if it survives incapacity.)

Until I am certified as incapacitated as provided hereunder, this Power of Attorney shall have no force or effect. All authority granted in this Power of Attorney shall be subject to establishment of incapacity as provided hereunder. After this Power of Attorney becomes effective, it shall not be affected by any subsequent incapacity which I may hereafter suffer or the passage of time. For purposes of establishing incapacity, whenever two licensed, practicing medical doctors who are not related to me or to any beneficiary or heir at law by blood or marriage certify in writing that I am unable to manage my financial affairs because of mental or physical infirmity and the certificates are personally served upon me, then the attorney(s)-in-fact named herein shall assume all powers granted in this Power of Attorney.

Anyone dealing with the attorney(s)-in-fact may rely upon written medical certificates or a photocopy of them presented to them along with the original Power of Attorney document, and shall incur no liability for any dealings with any designated attorney(s)-in-fact in good faith reliance on said certificate and the original Power of Attorney document. This provision is inserted in this document to encourage third parties to deal with my attorney(s)-in-fact without the need for court proceedings.

By way of illustration, but not limitation, I specifically authorize my attorney to do the following:

1. To ask, demand, sue for, recover, and receive all sums of money, debts, goods, merchandise, chattels, effects, and things of whatsoever nature or description which are now or hereafter shall be or become owing, due, payable, or belonging to me in or by any right whatsoever, and upon receipt thereof, to make, sign, execute, and deliver such receipts, releases, or other discharges for the same, respectively, as (s)he shall think fit.

2. To deposit any moneys which may come into his(her) hands as such attorney with any bank or bankers, either in my or his(her) own name, and any of such money or any other money to which I am entitled which now is or shall be so deposited to withdraw as (s)he shall think fit; to sign mutual savings bank and federal savings and loan association withdrawal orders; to sign and endorse checks payable to my order and to draw, accept, make, endorse, discount, or otherwise deal with any bills of exchange, checks, promissory notes, or other commercial or mercantile instruments; to borrow any sum or sums of money on such terms and with such security as he may think fit and for that purpose to execute all notes or other instruments which may be necessary or proper; and to have access to any and all safe deposit boxes registered in my name.

3. To sell, assign, transfer, and dispose of any and all stocks, bonds (including U.S. Savings Bonds), loans, mortgages, or other securities registered in my name; and to collect and receipt for all interest and dividends due and payable to me.

4. To invest in my name in any stock, shares, bonds (including U.S. Treasury Bonds referred to as "flower bonds"), securities, or other property, real or personal, and to vary such investments as (s)he, in his(her) sole discretion, may deem best; and to vote at meetings of shareholders or other meetings of any corporation or company and to execute any proxies or other instruments in connection therewith.

5. To enter into and upon my real estate, and to let, manage, and improve the same or any part thereof, and to repair or otherwise improve or alter, and to insure any buildings thereon; to sell, either at public or private sale or exchange, any part or parts of my real estate or personal property for such consideration and upon such terms as (s)he shall think fit, and to execute and deliver good and sufficient deeds or other instruments for the conveyance or transfer of the same, with such covenants of warranty or otherwise as (s)he shall see fit, and to give good and effectual receipts for all or any part of the purchase price or other consideration; and to mortgage my real estate and in connection therewith to execute bonds and warrants and all other necessary instruments and documents.

6. To contract with any person for leasing for such periods, at such rents and subject to such conditions as (s)he shall see fit, all or any of my said real estate; to give notice to quit to any tenant or occupier thereof; and to receive and recover from all tenants and occupiers thereof or of any part thereof all rents, arrears of rent, and sums of money which now are or shall hereafter become due and payable in respect thereof; and also on non-payment thereof or of any part thereof, to take all necessary or proper means and proceedings for determining the tenancy or occupation of such tenants or occupiers, and for ejecting the tenants or occupiers and recovering the possession thereof.

7. To commence, prosecute, discontinue, or defend all actions or other legal proceedings pertaining to me or my estate or any part thereof, to settle, compromise, or submit to arbitration any debt, demand, or other right or matter due me or concerning my estate as (s)he, in his sole discretion, shall deem best and for such purpose to execute and deliver such releases, discharges, or other instruments as (s)he may deem necessary and advisable; and to satisfy mortgages, including the execution of a good and sufficient release, or other discharge of such mortgage.

8. To prepare and file all income and other federal and state tax returns which the principal is required to file; to sign the principal's name to tax returns; hire preparers and advisors and pay for their services; and to do whatever is necessary to protect the principal's assets from assessments for income taxes and other taxes. The agent is specifically authorized to receive confidential information; to receive checks in payment of any refund of taxes, penalties, or interest; to execute waivers (including offers of waivers) of restrictions on assessment or collection of tax deficiencies and waivers of notice of disallowance of claims for credit or refund; to execute consents extending the statutory period for assessment or collection claims for credit or credit refund; to execute closing agreements under Internal Revenue Code section 7121, or any successor statute; and to delegate authority or substitute another representative with respect to all above matters.

9. To engage, employ, and dismiss any agents, clerks, servants, or other persons as (s)he, in his(her) sole discretion, shall deem necessary and advisable.

10. My agent has no authority to execute any trust instrument, or any document connected with the creation of a trust, or the amendment, modification, revocation (in whole or in part), or termination of an existing trust instrument to which I am a party.

11. To convey and transfer any of my property to trustees who shall hold the same for my benefit and/or the benefit of my children and other members of my immediate family upon such trust terms and conditions as to my attorney shall deem desirable.

12. To make gifts on the principal's behalf to a class composed of the principal's children, any of their issue, or both, to the full extent of the federal annual gift tax exclusion in effect from time to time, including the $15,000 per donee annual exclusion under Internal Revenue Code section 2503(b) or any successor statute, and for such purposes to remove the principal's assets from any grantor revocable trust of which the principal is a grantor.

13. To disclaim any interest in property for the purpose of making a qualified disclaimer within the meaning of section 2518 of the Internal Revenue Code.

14. To have access to all safe-deposit boxes in the principal's name or to which the principal is an authorized signatory; to contract with financial institutions for the maintenance and continuation of safe-deposit boxes in the principal's name; to add to and remove the contents of all such safe-deposit boxes; and to terminate contracts for all such safe-deposit boxes.

15. To use any credit cards in the principal's name to make purchases and to sign charge slips on behalf of the principal as may be required to use such credit cards; and to close the principal's charge accounts and terminate the principal's credit cards under circumstances where the agent considers such acts to be in the principal's best interest.

16. In general, to do all other acts, deeds, and matters whatsoever in or about my estate, property, and affairs as fully and effectually to all intents and purposes as I could do in my own proper person if personally present, giving to my said attorney power to make and substitute under him(her) an attorney or attorneys for all the purposes herein described, hereby ratifying and confirming all that the said attorney or substitute or substitutes shall do therein by virtue of these Presents.

17. In addition to the powers and discretion herein specially given and conferred upon my attorney, and notwithstanding any usage or custom to the contrary, to have the full power, right, and authority to do, perform, and to cause to be done and performed all such acts, deeds, and matters in connection with my property and estate as (s)he, in his(her) sole discretion, shall deem reasonable, necessary, and proper, as fully, effectually, and absolutely as if he were the absolute owner and possessor thereof.

18. When required to give reasonable effect to the context in which used, pronouns in the masculine, feminine, or neutral gender include each other, and nouns and pronouns in the plural or singular number include each other.

IN WITNESS HEREOF I have signed my name this _____ day of _____ 20_____ .

_____

Signature Witnessed:

_____

_____

STATE OF (   )
COUNTY OF (   ) On this _____ day of
_____ 20_____ .
Before me a Notary Public personally appeared
_____ known to me to be the person whose name is subscribed to this instrument and acknowledged that he/she executed it for the purposes herein expressed.

_____

_____
                    Notary

Durable Power of Attorney for Health Care

Notice to Person Making This Document
You have the right to make decisions about your health care. No health care may be given to you over your objection, and necessary health care may not be stopped or withheld if you object.

Because your health care providers in some cases may not have had the opportunity to establish a long-term relationship with you, they are often unfamiliar with your beliefs and values and the details of your family relationships. This poses a problem if you become physically or mentally unable to make decisions about your health care.

In order to avoid this problem, you may sign this legal document to specify the person whom you want to make health care decisions for you if you are unable to make those decisions personally. That person is known as your *health care agent*. You should take some time to discuss your thoughts and beliefs about medical treatment with the person or persons whom you have specified. You may state in this document any types of health care that you do or do not desire, and you may limit the authority of your health care agent. If your health care agent is unaware of your desires with respect to a particular health care decision, he or she is required to determine what would be in your best interest in making a decision.

This is an important legal document. It gives your agent broad powers to make health care decisions for you. It revokes any prior power of attorney for health care that you may have made. If you wish to change your Power of Attorney for Health Care, you may revoke this document at any time by destroying it, by directing another person to destroy it in your presence, by signing a written and dated statement of revocation, or by stating that it is revoked in the presence of two witnesses. If your agent is your spouse and your marriage is annulled or you are divorced after signing this document, the document is invalid.

Do not sign this document unless you clearly understand it. It is suggested that you keep a copy of this document on file with your physician.

Durable Power of Attorney for Health Care

Made this _____ day of _____, _____

Section 1
States Where This Document Is Effective

This Power of Attorney is intended to be effective in the following states: *Michigan, Wisconsin, Minnesota, Alabama, Arizona, Arkansas, California, Delaware, Florida, Georgia, Hawaii, Illinois, Indiana, Kansas, Kentucky, Massachusetts, Mississippi, Montana, Nebraska, Nevada, New Jersey, New Mexico, New York, North Carolina, North Dakota, Ohio, Oklahoma, Oregon, Pennsylvania, Rhode Island, South Dakota, Tennessee, Texas, and Virginia.* This document may also be effective in other states since it satisfies the witnessing requirements of all states and the District of Columbia. The law of the state in which this document is used shall be used to interpret and apply this document.

Section 2
Filing and Use of Document

A COPY OF YOUR HEALTH CARE POWER OF ATTORNEY/LIVING WILL SHOULD BE GIVEN TO YOUR ATTENDING PHYSICIAN. BRING A COPY OF THIS DOCUMENT WITH YOU EACH TIME YOU ARE ADMITTED TO A HOSPITAL.

I, _____, being of sound mind, intend by this document to create a power of attorney for health care. My executing this power of attorney for health care is voluntary. Despite the creation of this power of attorney for health care, I expect to be fully informed about and allowed to participate in any health care decision for me, to the extent that I am able. For the purposes of this document, "health care decision" means an informed decision to accept, maintain, discontinue, or refuse any care, treatment, service, or procedure to maintain, diagnose, or treat my physical or mental condition.

Section 3
Designation of Health Care Agent/Patient Advocate

If I am no longer able to make health care decisions for myself or cannot communicate health care decisions, due to incapacity, I hereby designate _____ to be my health care agent/patient advocate for the purpose of making health care decisions on my behalf. If I revoke my agent's authority or if my agent is not willing, able, or reasonably available to make a health care decision for me or cannot be contacted, I hereby designate _____ to be my alternate health care agent/patient advocate for the purpose of making health care decisions on my behalf.

Section 4
When Multiple Health Care Agents Are Appointed

When two or more agents/advocates are appointed at the same time, then the first appointed agent/advocate shall be the spokesperson and a health care provider can rely on the statements of the spokesperson, provided that such spokesperson shall consult with the other agents/advocates before making any decisions hereunder, provided that all appointed agents/advocates may take advocacy actions under Section 12 independently.

If a disagreement arises between agents/advocates appointed at the same time, then majority rules if there is an odd number of agents/advocates; and if there is an even number of agents/advocates then they shall resolve the disagreement among themselves in a friendly manner of mutual respect, but if they cannot, then the disagreement shall be mediated out of court, if possible, by a third party they select, and if this is unsuccessful, then a court of competent jurisdiction shall resolve the disagreement.

Section 5
Who Can Be My Health Care Agent

If permitted by applicable state law, any adult person I select may be appointed as my health care agent/patient advocate.

However, if applicable state law restricts whom I may appoint, then neither my health care agent/patient advocate nor my alternate health care agent/alternate patient advocate can be my present or former health care provider, an employee of my present or former health care provider, an employee of a health care facility in which I am or was a patient, an individual who makes the determination of my decision-making capacity, or a spouse of any of those persons, unless he or she is also my relative.

Section 6
When My Agent Can Act for Me

If permitted by applicable state law, I intend that this Power of Attorney shall be activated by only my attending physician who shall determine from a personal examination that I either lack the capacity to make my own health care decisions or cannot effectively communicate them.

If applicable state law requires the opinion of more than one professional to activate this Power of Attorney, then this Power of Attorney cannot be activated until my attending physician and another physician or a psychologist if permitted by applicable state law, who have personally examined me, have signed a statement that specifically expresses their opinions that I (a) lack capacity to make health care decisions, (b) am unable to receive and evaluate information effectively or to understand the significant benefits, risks, and alternatives to proposed health care, or (c) am unable to communicate health care decisions to such an extent that I lack the capacity to manage my health care decisions.

Provided, however, for purposes of allowing my agent/advocate to advocate for my health care needs under Paragraph 12, no professional determination of incapacity shall be required.

Section 7
General Statement of Authority Granted

I have completed and attached a Living Will providing specific direction to my agent/advocate. My agent/advocate is directed to implement those choices I have indicated in my attached Living Will. Unless I have specified otherwise in this document, or in the attached Living Will, if I am ever incapacitated, I instruct my health care provider to abide by the health care decisions of my agent/advocate, for all of my health care and treatment, even if such a decision could or would allow me to die. I have discussed my desires thoroughly with my agent/advocate and believe that he or she understands my philosophy regarding the health care decisions I would make if I were able. I desire that my wishes be carried out through the authority given to my agent/advocate under this document including the attached Living Will.

If I am unable, due to my incapacity, to make a health care decision, my health care agent/patient advocate is instructed to make the health care decisions for me. However, my health care agent/patient advocate should try to discuss with me any specific proposed health care if I can communicate in any manner, including by blinking my eyes. If I cannot communicate, my health care agent/patient advocate shall base his or her decision on any health care choices that I have expressed prior to my incapacity. If I have not expressed an opinion about the health care in question and I cannot communicate, my health care agent/patient advocate shall base his or her health care decision on what he or she believes to be in my best interest. Upon my death, my health care agent/patient advocate shall have control over my organs and my remains and is authorized to implement my expressed intent, if any, to donate my organs for the benefit of others. Nothing that I have stated herein shall be deemed to authorize my health care agent/patient advocate to consent to any form of assisted suicide.

My agent/advocate is authorized to take any action or make any decision permitted under applicable state law, e.g., a do-not-resuscitate order, if permitted by state law.

THIS POWER OF ATTORNEY IS *DURABLE* AND SHALL NOT BE AFFECTED BY MY DISABILITY.

Section 8
Limitations on Mental Health Treatment

My health care agent/patient advocate *may only* consent to my voluntary admission to an institution for mental diseases, an intermediate care facility for the mentally retarded, a state treatment facility, or a treatment facility if permitted by applicable state law. My health care agent/patient advocate *may only* consent to experimental mental health research or psychosurgery, electroconvulsive treatment, or drastic mental health treatment procedures for me if permitted by applicable state law.

Section 9
Limitations on Use During Pregnancy

If I am a woman, my health care agent/patient advocate may not make health care decisions for me if he/she knows that I am pregnant.

Section 10
Admission to Nursing Homes or Community-Based Residential Facilities

My health care agent/patient advocate may admit me to a nursing home or community-based residential facility for short-term stays for recuperative care or respite care. If I have checked *"Yes"* to the following, my health care agent/patient advocate has authority to *admit me* for long-term stays for recuperative care or respite care. If I have checked *"No"* to the following, my health care agent/patient advocate has no authority to ever admit me:

1. Authority to admit to a nursing home: Yes _____
No _____
2. Authority to admit to a community-based residential facility: Yes _____ No _____

Section 11
Provision of a Feeding Tube

If I have checked "*Yes*" to the following, my health care agent/
patient advocate *may have a feeding tube withheld or withdrawn* from me, unless my physician has advised that, in his
or her professional judgment, this will cause me pain or will
reduce my comfort. If I have checked "*No*" to the following, my
health care agent/patient advocate *may not have a feeding tube
withheld or withdrawn* from me unless my physician determines that a feeding tube would be medically ineffective.

Authority to withhold or withdraw a feeding tube:
Yes _____ No _____

Even though I have checked "yes" to the following, my agent/
advocate cannot have a feeding tube withheld or withdrawn if
my attending physician has advised that, in his or her professional judgment, such withholding or withdrawal will cause me
pain or reduce my comfort. My agent/advocate may not have
orally ingested nutrition or hydration withheld or withdrawn
from me unless provision of the nutrition or hydration is medically contraindicated (futile and hopeless).

Section 12
Power to Advocate and HIPAA Release

My agent/advocate appointed herein shall have these powers
to advocate for my health care needs without a professional
determination of incapacity, and this release applies to any
information governed by the Health Insurance Portability and
Accountability Act of 1996 (a/k/a HIPAA), 42 USC 1320d
and 45 CFR 160-164. I intend my agent/advocate to be treated
by health care providers, as required by HIPAA, as I would be
treated with respect to my rights regarding the use and disclosure of my identifiable protected health information or other
medical records. Pursuant to HIPAA, I authorize:

- any physician, health care professional, dentist, health
  plan, hospital, clinic, laboratory, pharmacy, or other
  covered health care provider, any insurance company,

and the Medical Information Bureau Inc., or other health care clearinghouse that has provided treatment or services to me or that has paid for or is seeking payment from me for such services to give, disclose, and release to my agent, without restriction, all of my individually identifiable health information and medical records regarding any past, present, or future medical or mental health condition, to include all information relating to the diagnosis and treatment of sexually transmitted diseases, mental illness, and drug or alcohol abuse.

The authority given to my agent shall supersede any prior agreement that I may have made with my health care providers to restrict access to or disclosure of my individually identifiable health information. The authority given to my agent has no expiration date and shall expire only in the event that I revoke the authority in writing and deliver it to my health care provider.

Further, I authorize my agent/advocate:

- To employ and discharge physicians, nurses, therapists, nurses' aides, and any other care providers, including, but not limited to, home health aides, domestic personal care providers, and chore-workers, as my agent/advocate may deem necessary and appropriate for my physical, mental, or emotional well-being;
- To give informed consent on my behalf with respect to any medical care, including diagnostic, surgical, therapeutic procedures, or other treatments of any type whether conventional or experimental;
- To consent to and to arrange administration of pain-relieving drugs or therapy; and
- To execute waivers, medical authorizations, and such other approval forms as may be required to permit or authorize care which I may need.

Section 13
Authorization to Attorney

I request and authorize my agent/advocate to employ the attorney who drafted this Power of Attorney or other attorney I employed in connection with my health care issues to assist in the interpretation and implementation of this Power of Attorney and my related Living Will.

Section 14
Reimbursement of Expenses

My agent/advocate shall be reimbursed for any expenses he/she incurs in connection with this Power of Attorney.

Section 15
Funeral Arrangements

My agent/advocate is authorized to take care of my funeral and burial arrangements and is directed to implement any pre-planned funeral and burial instructions that I have made.

All photocopies of this instrument shall have the same force and effect as the original.

(The principal and the witnesses all must sign this document at the same time.)

SIGNATURE OF PRINCIPAL
(Person Creating the Power of Attorney for Health Care)

Signature: _____ Date: _____

Print name _____

(The signing of this document by the principal revokes all previous powers of attorney for health care documents.)

STATEMENT OF WITNESSES

I declare under penalties of false swearing that I know the Principal personally and I believe her/him to be of sound mind and at least 18 years of age. I believe that the execution of this power of attorney for health care is voluntary. I am at least 18 years of age, am not related to the Principal by blood, marriage, or adoption, and am not directly financially responsible for the Principal's health care. I did not sign this document on behalf of the Principal. I am not a health care provider who is serving the Principal at this time or an employee of the health care provider (other than a chaplain or a social worker) of an inpatient health care facility in which the Principal is a patient. I am not the Principal's health care agent/patient advocate. To the best of my knowledge, I am not entitled to and do not have a claim to any part of the estate of the Principal upon death of the Principal under a will or trust now existing or by operation of law.

I was present when this was signed (or marked) and dated by the Principal. The Principal appeared to be of sound mind and free from duress.

Witness No. 1

(Print) Name: _____

Address: _____

Signature _____

Witness No. 2
(Print) Name: _____

Address: _____

Signature _____

State of _____

County of _____

NOTARY ACKNOWLEDGMENT

On this _____ day of _____, in the year 20_____ before me, the named notary, appeared the above-named Principal, _____, personally known to me (or proved to me on the basis of satisfactory evidence) to be the person whose name is subscribed to this instrument, and acknowledged that he or she executed it.

_____

Notary Acting in _____ County

ACCEPTANCE BY HEALTH CARE
AGENT/PATIENT ADVOCATE

I accept the designation as Health Care Agent/Patient Advocate for the Principal _____. I am at least 18 years of age and agree to the following terms. The Principal has discussed the Principal's wishes regarding health care decisions with me.

1. This designation shall not become effective unless the Principal is unable to participate in medical treatment decisions due to incapacity.

2. I cannot exercise powers concerning the Principal's care, custody, and medical treatment that the Principal, if the Principal were able to participate in the decision, could not have exercised on his or her own behalf.

3. This designation cannot be used to make a medical treatment decision to withhold or withdraw treatment from a Principal who is pregnant if that treatment would result in the pregnant Principal's death.

4. I may make a decision to withhold or withdraw treatment which would allow the Principal to die only if the Principal has expressed in a clear and convincing manner that I am authorized as health care agent/patient advocate to make such a decision, and that the Principal acknowledges that such a decision could or would allow the Principal's death. I understand that the language in the attached Living Will is a clear and convincing expression of my authority to make such decisions.

5. I shall not receive compensation for the performance of my authority, rights, and responsibilities, but I may be reimbursed for actual and necessary expenses incurred in the performance of my authority, rights, and responsibilities.

6. I shall act in accordance with the standards of care applicable to fiduciaries when acting for the Principal and shall act consistent with the Principal's best interests.

a. I shall take reasonable steps to follow the desires, instructions, or guidelines given by the Principal while the Principal was able to participate in care, custody, or medical treatment decisions, whether given orally, written in the attached Living Will, or as written in subsequent instructions.

b. The known desires of the Principal expressed or evidenced while the Patient was able to participate in medical treatment decisions are presumed to be in the Principal's best interests.

7. The Principal may revoke this designation at any time and in any manner sufficient to communicate an intent to revoke in accordance with the law of the state in which this document is used.

8. I may revoke my acceptance to this designation at any time and in any manner sufficient to communicate an intent to revoke.

9. A patient admitted to a health care facility or agency has the rights enumerated in Section 20201 of the Public Health Code, Act No. 368 of the Public Acts of 1978, being Section 333.20201 of the MCL and the rights set forth in the statutes of other states where this document is being used.

10. I may not delegate my powers to another individual without prior authorization by the Principal.

Agent's/Advocate's Signature:

_____

Address: _____

Telephone: _____

Alternate's Signature:

_____

Address: _____

Telephone: _____

This acceptance is not required by the law of all states.

Living Will and Declaration to Physicians

A Living Will is not a Last Will and Testament. It is a medical directive indicating the patient's desire as to the performance or non-performance of certain medical procedures. In the forms section, the Do Not Resuscitate order is a short version of these more detailed directions.

The interpretation and use of this Living Will shall be subject to my Durable Power of Attorney for Health Care, which is attached hereto, so that my physicians and other health care providers shall abide by the decisions of my Health Care Agent/ Patient Advocate.

Section 1
General Statement

I, _____, being of sound mind, voluntarily state my desire that my dying may not be prolonged under the circumstances specified in this document. Under those circumstances, I direct that I be permitted to die naturally. If I am unable to give directions regarding the use of life-sustaining procedures or feeding tubes, I intend that my family and physician honor this document as the final expression of my legal right to refuse medical or surgical treatment and to accept the consequences from this refusal, and I direct that the decision of my health care agent/patient advocate in interpreting my Living Will be binding on my physicians and family. If I have otherwise expressed my intent to be an organ donor, the need to preserve my organs to save another's life may be considered.

Section 2
When I Have a Terminal Condition

If I have a TERMINAL CONDITION, I do not want my dying to be artificially prolonged and I do not want life-sustaining procedures to be used. In addition, if I have such a terminal condition, the following are my directions regarding the use of feeding tubes:

2.1 Feeding Tubes (check only one):

    a. Use feeding tubes if I have a terminal condition _____

    b. Do not use feeding tubes if I have a terminal condition

    _____

Section 3
When I Am in a Persistent Vegetative State

If I am in a PERSISTENT VEGETATIVE STATE, the following are my directions regarding the use of life-sustaining procedures (check only one):

3.1 Life-Sustaining Procedures (check only one):

    a. Use life-sustaining procedures if I am in a persistent vegetative state _____

    b. Do not use life-sustaining procedures if I am in a persistent vegetative state _____

3.2 Feeding Tubes (check only one):

    a. Use feeding tubes if I am in a persistent vegetative state

    _____

    b. Do not use feeding tubes if I am in a persistent vegetative state _____

Section 4
Required Physician Determinations

If permitted by applicable state law, only the determination by my attending physician, who has personally examined me, that

I have a **terminal illness** or am in a **persistent vegetative state,** shall be required to honor my declarations as expressed above in Sections 2 and 3.

If applicable state law requires such determinations to be made by two physicians who have personally examined me, then my declarations expressed in Sections 2 and 3 cannot be honored until two physicians have made such determinations in compliance with applicable state law.

Section 5
Applicable Restrictions

5.1 If applicable state law mandates certain restrictions on my declarations on refusing medical treatment, then those restrictions shall apply. Specifically, if restricted by applicable state law, my declarations cannot authorize the withholding or withdrawal of any medication, life-sustaining procedure, or feeding tube, if such withholding or withdrawal will cause me pain or reduce my comfort, and such pain and discomfort cannot be alleviated through pain relief measures.

5.2 Any provision herein which violates applicable state law shall not apply.

5.3 With regard to nutrition and hydration, unless my attending physician advises that the administration of orally ingested nutrition and hydration is medically contraindicated (futile and hopeless), then I prefer receiving orally ingested nutrition and hydration when I am terminally ill or in a persistent vegetative state.

5.4 The withdrawal or withholding of life support cannot be authorized if I am known to be pregnant.

5.5 These declarations shall not be interpreted to permit assisted suicide.

Section 6
When Long-Term Care Is Needed

In the event that I need long-term care due to a permanent disability, it is my preference that I be allowed to remain at home if my health care agent/patient advocate believes that in-home care is feasible. If it is not in my best interest to remain at home, then it is my preference to remain in the least restrictive setting.

Section 7
Hospice and Palliative Care

I direct that hospice, pain medication, and palliative care be provided at all times, even if such treatment hastens my death.

Section 8
Organ and Tissue Donations

The following is my preference on donating my organs and tissue: Yes _____ No _____

Restrictions or specific limitations on organ donation if any are as follows:

_____

Section 9
Revocation

This document can be revoked as provided by the law of the state in which this document is used.

Signed:_____

Date: _____ 20_____

I declare under penalty of false swearing that I know the Principal personally and I believe her/him to be of sound mind and at least 18 years of age. I believe that the execution of this power of attorney for health care is voluntary. I am at least 18 years of age, am not related to the Principal by blood, marriage, or adoption, and am not directly financially responsible for the Principal's health care. I did not sign this document on behalf of the Principal. I am not a health care provider who is serving the Principal at this time or an employee of the health care provider (other than a chaplain or a social worker) of an inpatient health care facility in which the Principal is a patient.

I am not the Principal's health care agent/patient advocate. To the best of my knowledge, I am not entitled to and do not have a claim to any part of the estate of the Principal upon death of the Principal under a will or trust now existing or by operation of law.

I was present when this was signed (or marked) and dated by the Principal. The Principal appeared to be of sound mind and free from duress.

Witness: _____

Witness: _____

NOTARY ACKNOWLEDGMENT

On this _____ day of Witness: _____,
in the year 20___ before me, the named notary, appeared the above-named Principal, personally known to me (or proved to me on the basis of satisfactory evidence) to be the person whose name is subscribed to this instrument, and acknowledged that he or she executed it.

_____

Notary Public Acting in _____
County, State of _____

NOTE: THIS FORM CAN BE DUPLICATED AND A COPY SHALL BE GRANTED LEGAL EFFECT.

Certification from the Heir to a Vehicle

This is a Michigan form as an example of how a title to a boat or motor vehicle can get a title transferred without courts or lawyers. Other states have their own rules and procedures for transferring title where there is no probate.

The heir(s) must present a copy of the death certificate of the vehicle owner shown on the title.

When there is a secured party (lienholder) shown on the face of the title, a termination statement from the lienholder must be submitted.

I am the surviving spouse or the closest next of kin of the deceased whose death certificate is provided. I further certify the total value of all vehicles owned by the deceased does not exceed $60,000 and that the estate of the deceased is not being probated nor will it be probated in the future.

The vehicle title: ☐ is attached ☐ cannot be located

Vehicle Information	Death Certificate Information (Office Use Only)		
Year	Make	State	CountyBody Style
Docket Number		Vehicle Number	Date Examined
Branch Number		Title Number	Examiner (print)

I declare the statements above are true to the best of my knowledge.

Signature of Heir _____ Relationship to the Deceased _____

NOTE: Heir must complete odometer statement on title.

TRANSFER OF OWNERSHIP BY SURVIVING SPOUSE OR NEXT CLOSEST KIN

I, the surviving spouse, or if no surviving spouse, the next closest kin, certify the vehicle described above is sold or transferred to the person(s) named below and certify the title to be free of all previous liens:

New Owner(s)

Street Address City State Zip Code

Signature of Surviving Spouse or Next Closest Kin

_____

_____

Printed Name of Surviving Spouse or Next Closest Kin

IRA and Deferred Compensation Rollovers

Another disclaimer: The rules on rollovers and distribution from retirement plans are very complex and I strongly suggest going to your plan administrator for advice on how to handle your particular situation. The following is general information for educational purposes but may not apply to all types of retirement plans. No legal or tax advice is intended here. This information is courtesy of the IRS.

Most pre-retirement payments you receive from a retirement plan or IRA can be "rolled over" by depositing the payment in another retirement plan or IRA within sixty days. You can also have your financial institution or plan directly transfer the payment to another plan or IRA. The IRS has specific rules for inherited IRA's that depend upon your relationship to the deceased. Ask your broker or see this link: https://www.irs.gov/retirement-plans/plan-participant-employee/retirement-topics-beneficiary.

Why roll over?
When you roll over a retirement plan distribution, you generally don't pay tax on it until you withdraw it from the new plan. By rolling over, you're saving for your future and your money continues to grow tax-deferred.

If you don't roll over your payment, it will be taxable (other than qualified Roth distributions and any amounts already taxed) and you may also be subject to additional tax unless you're eligible for one of the exceptions to the 10 percent additional tax on early distributions.

How do I complete a rollover?

1. **Direct rollover**—If you're getting a distribution from a retirement plan, you can ask your plan administrator to make the payment directly to another retirement plan or to an IRA. Contact your plan administrator for instructions. The administrator may issue your distribution in the form of a check made payable to your new account. No taxes will be withheld from your transfer amount.

2. **Trustee-to-trustee transfer**—If you're getting a distribution from an IRA, you can ask the financial institution holding your IRA to make the payment directly from your IRA to another IRA or to a retirement plan. No taxes will be withheld from your transfer amount.

3. **Sixty-day rollover**—If a distribution from an IRA or a retirement plan is paid directly to you, you can deposit all or a portion of it in an IRA or a retirement plan within sixty days. Taxes will be withheld from a distribution from a retirement plan (see below), so you'll have to use other funds to roll over the full amount of the distribution.

When should I roll over?

You have sixty days from the date you receive an IRA or retirement plan distribution to roll it over to another plan or IRA. The IRS may waive the sixty-day rollover requirement in certain situations if you missed the deadline because of circumstances beyond your control.

IRA one-rollover-per-year rule

You generally cannot make more than one rollover from the same IRA within a one-year period. You also cannot make a rollover during this one-year period from the IRA to which the distribution was rolled over.

After January 1, 2015, you can make only one rollover from an IRA to another (or the same) IRA in any twelve-month period, regardless of the number of IRAs you own.

The one-per year limit does not apply to:

- rollovers from traditional IRAs to Roth IRAs (conversions)
- trustee-to-trustee transfers to another IRA
- IRA-to-plan rollovers
- plan-to-IRA rollovers
- plan-to-plan rollovers

Once this rule takes effect, the tax consequences are:

- you must include in gross income any previously untaxed amounts distributed from an IRA if you made an IRA-to-IRA rollover (other than a rollover from a traditional IRA to a Roth IRA) in the preceding twelve months, and
- you may be subject to the 10 percent early withdrawal tax on the amount you include in gross income.

See IRA One-Rollover-Per-Year Rule at www.irs.gov/retire-ment-plans/plan-participant-employee/rollovers-of-retire-ment-plan-and-ira-distributions for more on this limit.

Which types of distributions can I roll over?

IRAs: You can roll over all or part of any distribution from your IRA **except**:

1. A required minimum distribution or
2. A distribution of excess contributions and related earnings.

Retirement plans: You can roll over all or part of any distribution of your retirement plan account **except**:

1. Required minimum distributions,
2. Loans treated as a distribution,

3. Hardship distributions,
4. Distributions of excess contributions and related earnings,
5. A distribution that is one of a series of substantially equal payments,
6. Withdrawals electing out of automatic contribution arrangements,
7. Distributions to pay for accident, health or life insurance,
8. Dividends on employer securities, or
9. S corporation allocations treated as deemed distributions.

Distributions that can be rolled over are called "eligible rollover distributions." Of course, to get a distribution from a retirement plan, you have to meet the plan's conditions for a distribution, such as termination of employment.

Will taxes be withheld from my distribution?

- **IRAs**: An IRA distribution paid to you is subject to 10 percent withholding unless you elect out of withholding or choose to have a different amount withheld. You can avoid withholding taxes if you choose to do a trustee-to-trustee transfer to another IRA.

- **Retirement plans**: A retirement plan distribution paid to you is subject to mandatory withholding of 20 percent, even if you intend to roll it over later. Withholding does not apply if you roll over the amount directly to another retirement plan or to an IRA. A distribution sent to you in the form of a check payable to the receiving plan or IRA is not subject to withholding.

How much can I roll over if taxes were withheld from my distribution?

If you have not elected a direct rollover, in the case of a distribution from a retirement plan, or you have not elected out of withholding in the case of a distribution from an IRA, your plan administrator or IRA trustee will withhold taxes from your distribution. If you later roll the distribution over within sixty days, you must use other funds to make up for the amount withheld.

Example: Jordan, age forty-two, received a $10,000 eligible rollover distribution from her 401(k) plan. Her employer withheld $2,000 from her distribution.

1. If Jordan later decides to roll over the $8,000, but not the $2,000 withheld, she will report $2,000 as taxable income, $8,000 as a nontaxable rollover, and $2,000 as taxes paid. Jordan must also pay the 10 percent additional tax on early distributions on the $2,000 unless she qualifies for an exception.
2. If Jordan decides to roll over the full $10,000, she must contribute $2,000 from other sources. Jordan will report $10,000 as a nontaxable rollover and $2,000 as taxes paid.

If you roll over the full amount of any eligible rollover distribution you receive (the actual amount received plus the 20 percent that was withheld—$10,000 in the example above):

- Your entire distribution would be tax-free, and
- You would avoid the 10 percent additional tax on early distributions.

What happens if I don't make any election regarding my retirement plan distribution?

The plan administrator must give you a written explanation of your rollover options for the distribution, including your right to have the distribution transferred directly to another retirement plan or to an IRA.

If you're no longer employed by the employer maintaining your retirement plan and your plan account is between $1,000 and $5,000, the plan administrator may deposit the money into an IRA in your name if you don't elect to receive the money or roll it over. If your plan account is $1,000 or less, the plan administrator may pay it to you, less, in most cases, 20 percent income tax withholding, without your consent. You can still roll over the distribution within sixty days.

Which retirement accounts can accept rollovers?
You can roll your money into almost any type of retirement plan or IRA.

Is my retirement plan required to allow transfer of any amounts eligible for a distribution?
If you receive an eligible rollover distribution from your plan of $200 or more, your plan administrator must provide you with a notice informing you of your rights to roll over or transfer the distribution and must facilitate a direct transfer to another plan or IRA.

Is my retirement plan required to accept rollover contributions?
Your retirement plan is not required to accept rollover contributions. Check with your new plan administrator to find out if they are allowed and, if so, what type of contributions are accepted.

Required Minimum Distributions

You cannot keep retirement funds in your account indefinitely. You generally have to start taking withdrawals from your IRA, SIMPLE IRA, SEP IRA, or retirement plan account when you reach age 70½. However, changes were made by the Setting Every Community Up for Retirement Enhancement (SECURE) Act, which was part of the Further Consolidated Appropriations Act, 2020, P.L. 116-94, signed by the president on December 20, 2019. Due to changes made by the SECURE Act, if your seventieth birthday is July 1, 2019 or later, you do not have to take withdrawals until you reach age seventy-two. Roth IRAs do not require withdrawals until after the death of the owner.

Your **required minimum distribution** is the minimum amount you must withdraw from your account each year.

- You can withdraw more than the minimum required amount.
- Your withdrawals will be included in your taxable income except for any part that was taxed before (your basis) or that can be received tax-free (such as qualified distributions from designated Roth accounts).

Do these rules apply to my retirement plan?
The minimum distribution rules discussed below apply to:
- traditional IRAs
- SEP IRAs

- SIMPLE IRAs
- 401(k) plans
- 403(b) plans
- 457(b) plans
- profit sharing plans
- other defined contribution plans

Calculating the required minimum distribution
The required minimum distribution for any year is the account balance as of the end of the immediately preceding calendar year divided by a distribution period from the IRS's "Uniform Lifetime Table." A separate table is used if the sole beneficiary is the owner's spouse who is ten or more years younger than the owner. In this regard, the following materials will be useful to you in determining required distribution amounts and payout periods:

- worksheets to calculate the required amount
- tables to calculate the RMD during the participant or IRA owner's life:
  - Uniform Lifetime Table—for all unmarried IRA owners calculating their own withdrawals, married owners whose spouses aren't more than ten years younger, and married owners whose spouses aren't the sole beneficiaries of their IRAs
  - Table I (Single Life Expectancy) is used for beneficiaries who are not the spouse of the IRA owner
  - Table II (Joint Life and Last Survivor Expectancy) is used for owners whose spouses are more than ten years younger and are the IRA's sole beneficiaries

Inherited IRAs—If your IRA or retirement plan account was inherited from the original owner, see "Required minimum distributions after the account owner dies," below.

Beginning date for your first required minimum distribution (RMD)

- **IRAs (including SEPs and SIMPLE IRAs)**
  - April 1 of the year following the calendar year in which you reach age 70½, if you were born before July 1, 1949.
  - April 1 of the year following the calendar year in which you reach age 72, if you were born after Jun 30, 1949.
- **401(k), profit-sharing, 403(b), or other defined contribution plan**
- Generally, April 1 following the later of the calendar year in which you:
  - reach age 72 (age 70½ if born before July 1, 1949), or
  - retire (if your plan allows this).

See the chart (at https://www.irs.gov/retirement-plans/ rmd-comparison-chart-iras-vs-defined-contribution-plans) comparing IRA and defined contribution plan RMDs.

Date that you turn 70½ (72 if you reach the age of 70½ after December 31, 2019):

You reach age 70½ on the date that is six calendar months after your 70th birthday.

Example: You are retired and your 70th birthday was June 30, 2018. You reached age 70½ on December 30, 2018. You must take your first RMD (for 2018) by April 1, 2019. You will take subsequent RMDs on December 31st annually thereafter, as will be discussed below.

Example: You are retired and your 70th birthday was July 1, 2019. You reach age 70½ after December 31, 2019, so you are not required to take a minimum distribution until you reach 72. You reached age 72 on July 1, 2021. You must take your first RMD (for 2021) by April 1, 2022, with subsequent RMDs on December 31st annually thereafter.

Terms of the plan govern
A plan may require you to begin receiving distributions by April 1 of the year after you reach age 70½ (age 72 if born after June 30, 1949), even if you have not retired.

5 percent owners
If you own more than 5 percent of the business sponsoring the plan, then you must begin receiving distributions by April 1 of the year after the calendar year in which you reach age 70½ (age 72 if born after June 30, 1949), even if you have not retired.

Date for receiving subsequent required minimum distributions
For each year after your required beginning date, you must withdraw your RMD by December 31.

For the first year following the year you reach age 70½ (age 72 if born after June 30, 1949), you will generally have two required distribution dates: an April 1 withdrawal (for the year you turn 70½ (or 72 if born after June 30, 1949)) and an additional withdrawal by December 31 (for the year following the year you turn 70½ (or 72 if born after June 30, 1949)). You can make your first withdrawal by December 31 of the year you turn 70½ (or 72 if born after June 30, 1949) instead of waiting until April 1 of the following year, which would allow the distributions to be included in your income in separate tax years.

Example: John reached age 70½ on August 20, 2019. He must receive his 2019 required minimum distribution by April 1, 2020, based on his 2019 year-end balance. John must receive his 2020 required minimum distribution by December 31, 2020, based on his 2020 year-end balance.

If John receives his initial required minimum distribution for 2019 on December 31, 2019, then he will take the first RMD in 2019 and the second in 2020. However, if John waits to take his first RMD until April 1, 2020, then both his 2019 and 2020 distributions will be included in income on his 2020 income tax return.

Example: Paul reached age 70½ on January 28, 2020. Since Paul had not reached age 70½ before 2020, his first RMD is due for 2021, the year he turns 72. Paul's first RMD is due by April 1, 2022, based on his 2020 year-end balance. Paul must receive his 2022 required minimum distribution by December 31, 2022, based on his 2021 year-end balance.

Consequence for failing to take required minimum distributions

If you do not take any distributions, or if the distributions are not large enough, you may have to pay a 50 percent excise tax on the amount not distributed as required.

- To report the excise tax, you may have to file Form 5329, Additional Taxes on Qualified Plans (Including IRAs) and Other Tax-Favored Accounts.
- See the Form 5329 instructions PDF (at https://www.irs.gov/pub/irs-pdf/i5329.pdf) for additional information about this tax.

Required minimum distributions after the account owner dies

For the year of the account owner's death, use the RMD the account owner would have received. For the year following the owner's death, the RMD will depend on the identity of the designated beneficiary.

Calculating required minimum distributions for designated beneficiaries

Generally, for individuals or employees with accounts who die prior to January 1, 2020, designated beneficiaries of retirement accounts and IRAs calculate RMDs using the Single Life Table (Table I, Appendix B, IRS Publication 590-B, Distributions from Individual Retirement Arrangements (IRAs)). The table provides a life expectancy factor based on the beneficiary's age. The account balance is divided by this life expectancy factor to determine the first RMD. The life expectancy is reduced by one for each subsequent year.

If the distribution is from a qualified retirement plan, the plan document will establish the RMD rules, and the plan administrator should provide the beneficiary with his or her options. The options for the RMD pay-out period may be as short as five years, or as long as the life expectancy of the beneficiary. (If the beneficiary is the spouse of the owner, the spouse can also choose to treat the IRA as his or her own.) Therefore, if the distribution is from a qualified plan, the beneficiary should contact the plan administrator. For IRA distributions, see Publication 590-B, Distribution from Individual Retirement Arrangements (IRAs).

Generally, for individuals or employees with accounts who die after December 31, 2019, the SECURE Act distinguishes between an "eligible designated beneficiary" and other beneficiaries who inherit an account or IRA. An eligible designated beneficiary includes a surviving spouse, a disabled individual, a chronically ill individual, a minor child, or an individual who is not more than ten years younger than the account owner. Certain trusts created for the exclusive benefit of disabled or chronically ill beneficiaries are included. These eligible designated beneficiaries may take their distributions over the beneficiary's life expectancy. However, minor children must still take remaining distributions within ten years of reaching age eighteen. Additionally, a surviving spouse beneficiary may delay commencement of distributions until the later of the end of the year that the employee or IRA owner would have attained age seventy-two, or the surviving spouse's required beginning date.

Designated beneficiaries, who are not an eligible designated beneficiary, must withdraw the entire account by the tenth calendar year following the year of the employee or IRA owner's post-2019 death. Non-designated beneficiaries must withdraw the entire account within five years of the employee or IRA owner's death if distributions have not begun prior to death. For IRA distributions, see IRS Publication 590-B, Distribution from Individual Retirement Arrangements (IRAs).

Social Security Survivors' Benefits

This information is from the Social Security website.
You should let Social Security know as soon as possible when a person in your family dies. Usually, the funeral director will report the person's death to Social Security. You'll need to give the deceased's Social Security number to the funeral director so he or she can make the report. Some of the deceased's family members may be able to receive Social Security benefits if the deceased person worked long enough in jobs insured under Social Security to qualify for benefits. Contact Social Security as soon as you can to make sure the family gets all the benefits they're entitled to. Please read the following information from the Social Security Administration carefully to learn what benefits may be available.

- We can pay a one-time payment of $255 to the surviving spouse if the spouse was living with the deceased. If living apart and eligible for certain Social Security benefits on the deceased's record, the surviving spouse may still be able to get this one-time payment. If there's no surviving spouse, a child who's eligible for benefits on the deceased's record in the month of death can get this payment.
- Certain family members may be eligible to receive monthly benefits, including:

A widow or widower age sixty or older (age fifty or older if disabled);

A widow or widower any age caring for the deceased's child who is under age sixteen or disabled;

An unmarried child of the deceased who is: younger than age eighteen (or up to age nineteen if they're a full-time student in an elementary or secondary school); or age eighteen or older with a disability that began before age twenty-two;

A stepchild, grandchild, step grandchild, or adopted child under certain circumstances; Parents, age sixty-two or older, who were dependent on the deceased for at least half of their support; and

A surviving divorced spouse, under certain circumstances.

If the deceased was receiving Social Security benefits, you must return the benefit received for the month of death or any later months. For example, if the person dies in July, you must return the benefit paid in August. If received by direct deposit, contact the bank or other financial institution and ask them to return any funds received for the month of death or later. If paid by check, do not cash any checks received for the month the person dies or later. Return the checks to Social Security as soon as possible. However, eligible family members may be able to receive death benefits for the month the beneficiary died.

Contacting Social Security

The most convenient way to contact us anytime, anywhere is to visit www.socialsecurity.gov. There, you can: apply for benefits; open a My Social Security account, which you can use to review your Social Security Statement, verify your earnings, print a benefit verification letter, change your direct deposit information, request a replacement Medicare card, and get a replacement SSA-1099/1042S; obtain valuable information; find publications; get answers to frequently asked questions; and much more. If you don't have access to the Internet, we offer many automated services by telephone, twenty-four hours a day, seven days a week. Call us toll-free at (800) 772-1213 or at our TTY number, (800) 325-0778, if you're deaf or hard of hearing. If you need to speak to a person, we can answer your calls from 7:00 a.m. to 7:00 p.m., Monday through Friday. We ask for your patience during busy periods since you may experience a higher than usual rate of busy signals and longer hold times to speak to us. We look forward to serving you.

Department of Veterans Affairs Benefits

This information is verbatim from the VA website. I can't explain it better than this:

Burial Benefits, Death Benefits, and Memorial Items for Veterans

Veterans can receive military funeral honors and memorial items whether they're interred in a veterans cemetery or a private one.

If you're a veteran and your discharge was not dishonorable, you can probably be buried in a national veterans cemetery. Arlington National Cemetery has stricter eligibility rules than other national cemeteries.

Military Funeral Honors and Memorial Items

Almost all veterans can receive military funeral honors at no cost. They are also usually eligible for free memorial items including:

- Headstones, markers, and medallions
- Burial flag
- Presidential Memorial Certificate

Learn how to apply for veterans memorial items.

Veterans Burial Benefits and Death Benefits at Private Cemeteries

Veterans buried in private cemeteries can receive military funeral honors and memorial items.

The veteran's family or representative can apply for a veterans burial allowance (or veterans death benefit), in certain cases. These include veterans receiving a VA pension or compensation. The burial allowance can help pay for burial, funeral, and transportation costs. It can't be used for cremation, which is a funeral director service.

Eligibility for Burial in National and State Veterans Cemeteries

VA National Cemeteries

Eligibility for burial in a VA national cemetery is typically open to a:

- Veteran of the armed forces
- Service member who died while on active duty
- Veteran's spouse
- Veteran's minor child

See an interactive map and list of Department of Veterans Affairs (VA) national cemeteries.

Apply in advance to learn if you qualify for burial in a VA national cemetery. If you do qualify, you'll get the confirmation in a pre-need decision letter.

Arlington National Cemetery

Eligibility for Arlington National Cemetery is different. Only active duty, military retirees, former prisoners of war, and recipients of the Purple Heart and other top awards can be buried there. But other veterans may be eligible for above-ground inurnment.

Spouses and minor children of eligible service members and veterans can be buried at Arlington, too.

State Veterans Cemeteries

Requirements for burial in a state veterans cemetery are like those for VA cemeteries. They may also have residency requirements.

See a list of state and territory veterans cemeteries.

Schedule a Burial for a Veteran or Family Member

Schedule a Burial at a National Cemetery

If the veteran or spouse confirmed their eligibility in advance and received a pre-need decision letter, call the National Cemetery Scheduling Office at (800) 535-1117 to start your request.

If eligibility was not pre-determined, that will have to happen first. See the steps for scheduling a burial at a VA national cemetery.

Schedule a Burial at Arlington National Cemetery

To schedule a burial at Arlington National Cemetery, call the ANC customer service center: (877) 907-8585.

Schedule a Burial at a State Veterans Cemetery

The VA does not manage burials at state, territorial, or tribal veterans cemeteries. Contact the cemetery directly.

Life Insurance and Survivor Benefits for Service Members and Veterans

Get information on military life insurance. Learn how your family can get survivor benefits, sometimes called death benefits.

SGLI and VGLI Life Insurance

- Active Duty: If you're in the military, you're automatically signed up for Servicemembers' Group Life Insurance (SGLI).
- Veterans: You can sign-up for Veterans' Group Life Insurance (VGLI) for a limited time after you're discharged.

Survivor Benefits Plans for Military Retirees

Your pension ends when you die unless you sign up for a survivor (death) benefit plan when you retire. The plan offers a monthly annuity for your survivors.

- Active-duty retirees can enroll in the military's Survivor Benefit Plan (SBP).
- Reserve and National Guard retirees can enroll in the Reserve Component Survivor Benefit Plan (RCSBP).

If you're the survivor of a:

- Department of Defense military retiree, report the death to the Defense Finance and Accounting Service (DFAS)
- Coast Guard retiree, contact the Coast Guard Pay & Personnel Center

Benefits for Survivors of Veterans

You may qualify for death benefits from the VA if you are the survivor of a:

- Service member or veteran whose death was service-connected
- Veteran whose total disability was service-connected but their death was not

Deactivating or Memorializing Digital Presence

Deactivating or memorializing Facebook accounts
From Facebook:

> Choose someone to look after your account after you pass away. They will be able to:
> - Manage tribute posts to your profile, which includes deciding who can post and who can see posts, deleting posts, and removing tags
> - Request the removal of your account
> - Respond to new friend requests
> - Update your profile picture and cover photo
>
> Your legacy contact can only manage posts made after you've passed away. They won't be able to post as you or see your messages.
>
> We'll let your legacy contact know that you chose them. They won't be notified again until your account is memorialized.
>
> If you don't want a Facebook account after you pass away, you can request to have your account permanently deleted instead of choosing a legacy contact.

Instagram accounts
These can likewise be **removed or memorialized**. You will need to provide a death certificate, birth certificate, and proof that you are the person in charge of the estate. This could be your

Letters of Authority from the probate court, or an affidavit of trust showing you as the successor trustee of the trust. The online form reads as follows:

> Please use this form to request the removal of a deceased person's account. We extend our condolences and appreciate your patience and understanding throughout this process.
>
> You will be asked for the following: Your Name, your email address, full name of the deceased person, username of the deceased person's email account, a link to the Instagram account of the deceased person, and when did they pass away.
>
> You'll need to upload documentation like a death certificate, the deceased person's birth certificate or proof of authority
>
> Request to Memorialize a Deceased Person's Instagram Account
>
> After someone has passed away, we'll memorialize their account if a family member or friend submits a request. If you'd like a loved one's account to be memorialized, please use this form to let us know.
>
> Memorialized accounts are a place to remember someone's life after they've passed away. Memorialized accounts on Instagram have the following key features:
> - No one can log into a memorialized account.
> - The word **Remembering** will be shown next to the person's name on their profile.
> - Posts the deceased person shared, including photos and videos, stay on Instagram and are visible to the audience they were shared with.
> - Memorialized accounts don't appear in certain places on Instagram, like Explore.
>
> Once memorialized, no one will be able to make changes to any of the account's existing posts or information. This means no changes to the following:
> - Photos or videos added by the person to their profile.
> - Comments on posts shared by the person to their profile.
> - Privacy settings of their profile.

- The current profile photo, followers or people the person follows.

If you feel that a post or comment on a memorialized profile doesn't follow our Community Guidelines or Terms of Use, you may report it with the report feature located next to the post or next to the comment.

Deactivating Twitter accounts

The process is easier if you can access their account with a password. Here is the information from Twitter as to the deactivation process either with the password or without:

All the information you'll need to delete a Twitter account.

How to Delete an Account:

1. Log in to Twitter from a desktop or mobile browser.

2. Click the gear icon at the upper right and select "Settings."

3. Scroll down to the bottom of the page and click "Deactivate my account."

4. Read the account deactivation information, then click "Okay, fine, deactivate account."

5. Enter password.

The account will officially be deleted 30 days after the request, during which time the account can be reactivated by logging in.

Required Information

- *Email*
- *Password*

*How to Deactivate or Delete a Twitter Account **If You Don't Have the Required Information** Listed Above*

According to Twitter's Help Section:

In the event of the death of a Twitter user, we can work with a person authorized to act on the behalf of the estate or with a verified immediate family member of the deceased to have an account deactivated. The following information is required:

1. *The username of the deceased user's Twitter account (e.g., @username or twitter.com/username)*

2. *A copy of the deceased user's death certificate*

3. *A copy of your government-issued ID (e.g., driver's license)*

4. *A signed statement including:*

- *Your first and last name*
- *Your email address*
- *Your current contact information*
- *Your relationship to the deceased user or their estate*
- *Action requested (e.g., "Please deactivate the Twitter account")*
- *A brief description of the details that evidence this account belongs to the deceased, if the name on the account does not match the name on death certificate.*
- *A link to an online obituary or a copy of the obituary from a local newspaper (optional)*

Please send us the documentation by fax or mail to the following address:

Twitter, Inc.

c/o: Trust & Safety

1355 Market St., Suite 900

San Francisco, CA 94103

Fax: (415) 865-5405

Note: *This is a United States number, so please be sure to include the appropriate international dialing code if you're sending from outside the United States.*

We conduct all of our communication via email; should we require any other information, we will contact you at the email address you have provided in your request. If you have any questions, you can contact us at: privacy@twitter.com.

Please note: *We (Twitter) are unable to provide account access to anyone regardless of his or her relationship to the deceased (if you do not have the password.)*

Assets Checklist

Assets. Include the location of the assets and any supporting documents such as deeds or titles as well as account numbers and the contact information for any agent or company, broker or bank involved. Values are estimates.

Real Estate: Home   _____
   Vacation Home   _____
   Other   _____
Vehicles: Cars   _____
Boats   _____
   Motor Home   _____
Investments: IRA's   _____
   Money Market   _____
   Stocks/Bonds   _____
   Other Tax Deferred   _____
Pension/Stock options   _____
Cash Accounts: Savings   _____
   Average Checking   _____
   Gold/Precious metals   _____
   Broker Accounts   _____
Insurance: Life (face amount)   _____
   Annuities   _____
   Prepaid burial   _____
Miscellaneous: Jewelry   _____

Collections   _____

Antiques   _____

Receivables   _____

Expected inheritances   _____

Business Interests   _____

Household Goods   _____

Safe deposit boxes or storage units. Including location of keys to same Other assets

Index

 **Books
from
Allworth
Press**

Estate Planning for the Healthy, Wealthy Family
by Carla Garrity, Mitchell Baris, and Stanley Neeleman (6 × 9, 256 pages, ebook, $22.99)

Estate Planning (in Plain English)°
by Leonard D. DuBoff and Amanda Bryan (6 × 9, 240 pages, paperback, $19.99)

Feng Shui and Money (Second Edition)
by Eric Shaffert (6 × 9, 256 pages, paperback, $19.99)

How to Avoid Probate for Everyone
by Ronald Farrington Sharp (5½ × 8¼, 192 pages, paperback $16.99)

How to Plan and Settle Estates
by Edmund Fleming (6 × 9, 288 pages, paperback, $16.95)

Legal Forms for Everyone (Sixth Edition)
by Carl Battle (8½ × 11, 280 pages, paperback, $24.99)

Living Trusts for Everyone (Second Edition)
by Ronald Farrington Sharp (5½ × 8¼, 192 pages, paperback $16.99)

Legal Guide to Social Media
by Kimberly A. Houser (6 × 9, 208 pages, paperback, $19.95)

Love & Money
by Ann-Margaret Carrozza with foreword by Dr. Phil McGraw (6 × 9, 240 pages, paperback, $19.99)

The Money Mentor
by Tad Crawford (6 × 9, 272 pages, paperback, $24.95)

Protecting Your Assets from Probate and Long-Term Care
by Evan H. Farr (6 × 9, 208 pages, paperback, $14.99)

Scammed
by Gini Graham Scott, PhD (6 × 9, 256 pages, paperback, $14.99)

The Secret Life of Money
by Tad Crawford (5½ × 8½, 304 pages, paperback, $19.95)

The Smart Consumer's Guide to Good Credit
by John Ulzheimer (5¼ × 8¼, 216 pages, paperback, $14.95)

Your Living Trust & Estate Plan (Fifth Edition)
by Harvey J. Platt (6 × 9, 352 pages, paperback, $16.95)

To see our complete catalog or to order online, please visit *www.allworth.com*.